MW01243586

COVER PHOTOS: (Clockwise from lower left)
"Anna's Frame"—Chapter 3; "Mary At My Window Watching"—Chapter 6; Example of "The Angel of O.L.A."—Chapter 9; Our Lady of Lourdes Grotto of the Southwest, Spiritual Center of the Oblates of Mary Immaculate of the Southern U S Province from "San Antonio Pickup"—Chapter 13. (In the Center: the CHI RHO, the first two letters of Christ in Greek, symbolizing God as the source of all miracles.)

THE MIRACLE MAKERS

by
Mary Talken

MIRACULOUS STORIES, PRAYER & PRAISE

A GOLDEN FRAME PUBLICATION

Published in the United States by Mary Talken

The extraordinary incidents expressed in this book fall in the theological area that deals with mystical phenomena and are based solely on human credibility and should not be viewed with divine faith. Although we are free to write and discuss supernatural experiences in the lives of the faithful, we also relinquish final judgment regarding these incidents to the official teachings and/or recommendations of the Roman Catholic Church.

If any copyrighted materials have been inadvertently used in this work without proper credit being given, please notify Mary Talken in writing so any future printings of this work may be corrected accordingly.

Grateful acknowledgment is made to the following for permission to reprint previously published materials:

All Scripture quotations (with the exception of those noted in the story, "A New Heart For Debbie") are taken from *THE NEW AMERICAN BIBLE,* copyright, 1970. Used by permission.

Scripture quotes in "A New Heart For Debbie" are taken from the New King James Version. Copyright © 1979, 1980, 1982 by Thomas Nelson, Inc. Used by permission. All rights reserved.

"The Beginning-Tim's Story" is from the book *WHERE ANGELS WALK: TRUE STORIES OF HEAVENLY VISITORS* by Joan Wester Anderson. Copyright © 1992 by Joan Wester Anderson. Published by Barton & Brett, Publishers, Inc. Reprinted by permission.

Various quotes taken from *QUIPS, QUOTES AND QUESTS* by Vern McLellan. Copyright © 1992 by Harvest House Publishers, Eugene, Oregon. Used by permission. 1.

What angels would say in Chapter 10 reprinted by permission of Warner Books, Inc. New York, U.S.A. From *"Touched By Angels"* by Eileen Elias Freeman. Copyright 1995. All rights reserved.

Explanation of church views and faith in the Introduction are taken from *VOICES, VISIONS AND APPARITIONS* by Michael Freze, S.F.O. Copyright 1992 by Michael Freze, S.F.O. Our Sunday Visitor Publishing Division, Huntington, Indiana. Used by permission.

THE MIRACLE MAKERS, Miraculous Stories, Prayer & Praise

Mary Talken
ISBN #0-9619510-3-6 (Paperback)
ISBN #0-9619510-4-4 (Hardcover)

PRINTED IN THE UNITED STATES

CONTENTS

ACKNOWLEDGMENTS

This book is a miracle in its existence. As editor-in-chief, God required the use of our hands and feet in order to bring it to life. Thank you, Lord, for the opportunity to serve you.

Because it is a rare book that doesn't depend on information already recorded somewhere, sometime in the past, I wish to thank all whose words on this topic may have prompted anything found herein for the greater glory of God. This book's profits will go to His works.

My own deepest personal and heartfelt thanks to a great Company of fine contributors who so willingly shared their treasured stories. Without their faith and confidence in me, these wonders would still lie hidden from a faith-hungry world. Although most of these stories come from Christian people of the Roman Catholic tradition, this work is ecumenical and includes stories from other wonderful Christians who represent several denominations. This writer is and will forever be grateful for the trust they have shown in her and the project. There is, of course, no implication that all who have contributed stories are in agreement with the total contents, opinions or statements expressed.

These fine people include: Father Pedro (Pierre) Amen, Rev. Lee & Lavon Amsler, Joan Wester Anderson, Joseph Bonansinga, Ann & Jeff Bradshaw, Billie Brod, Brian Brod, Barbara and Duke Curran, Marcella Davis, Virginia Drew, Jan Faler, Sue Finley, Gloria Gebhardt, Betty Geisendorfer, Rita Goerlich, Clairice Hetzler, Sharon Kay, Bill and Loretta Kimminau, Julia, Peg Markle, Pat McCarthy, Pat Middendorf, Carol Oliver, Genevia Osborne, Peggy Phillips, Ella Marie Reiter, Leona Richardet, Edna Runser, Leanne Schell, Don Schulte, Ed J. and Marilyn Schumer, Sharon Seuferer, Carmela Simone, Ida "Burny" Smith, Carlene Soebbing, Bonnie Brod-Stickney, Bob Wensing, Carolyn Witsken, Sharon Zehnle.

My grateful appreciation and thanks for the professional advice and assistance of Katheryn Ullmen, Jack Inghram, Barbara Brett of Barton & Brett Publishing, Joan Wester Anderson, Rev. Roy Bauer, Father John Carberry, Sister Elizabeth Mast, S.P.F., Harvest House and Verne McLellan, Our Sunday Visitor and Michael Freze S.F.O., Warner Books and Eileen Elias Freeman, the United States Catholic Conference and Thomas Nelson,

Inc. for permission to use Scriptural quotations, and Father Richard A. Houlahan, O.M.I.

Last but not least, my special thanks to my dear husband Larry, my family and the friends who supported me in this endeavor, as well as all those who supported our contributors.

INTRODUCTION

What is a miracle? Quite simply, it is something wonderful and marvelous that happens contrary to the rules of nature and science, a temporary suspension of one of its laws. It does not happen by accident, and if it can be easily explained, it is no miracle.

But when a miracle actually occurs, the recipient experiences God's loving intervention through some obvious change, the resolution to a difficult situation, the actual appearance of a heavenly being (the Miracle Makers), dreams, premonitions, warnings or inner voices. Each time a miraculous event takes place, the favored soul is usually aware that something unusual and divine is happening, and is left feeling refreshed, joy-filled and warm with an inner glow.

So, who are these Miracle Makers? Quite simply and beautifully, they are Heaven's residents.

The Main Miracle Maker is awesome beyond all imagination, all-powerful, all-merciful and He presides over his kingdom from a magnificent throne. It is through his wisdom, his permission and his presence in them that the other Miracle Makers can complete their earthly missions. We address this Mighty Monarch as **GOD (the Father, Son and Holy Spirit).**

The second Miracle Maker is a mystical lady, crowned Queen of Heaven and Earth. Once she shared our human nature; now she understands our needs and often appears to us in a variety of mantles, veils and gowns when delivering messages, miracles and warnings to her earthly children. We love and venerate her, the **BLESSED VIRGIN MARY.**

The third group of Miracle Makers is brilliant. They worship and sing God's praises around His heavenly throne while displaying a preference for long flowing white gowns and for flying, which accounts for any feathered appendages seen on these busy messengers known as **ANGELS.**

The fourth group of Miracle Makers are those special human beings of exceptional virtue who have died and have been officially recognized by the Church as having reached a glorified state in Heaven. Because they are so close to God, we pray for their intercession, the intercession of the **SAINTS.***

Working together, these Miracle Makers perform spiritual acts every day of the year. After all, Jesus performed so many miracles while He lived on earth that John admits in Jn.21:25, "There are still many other things that Jesus did, yet if they were written about in detail, I doubt there would be room enough in the entire world to hold the books to record them."

Since the Church always exercises prudence and caution in dealing with spiritual phenomena, we have made every effort to present our stories with truth and accuracy of fact according to Church teachings.

Pope Urban VIII (1623–1644) once declared, "In those cases which concern private revelations, it is better to believe than not believe, for if it is proven true, you will be happy that you believed because our Holy Mother asked it. If you believe and it should be proven false, you will receive all the blessings as if it had been true because you believed it to be true."

Yes, when it comes to believing or not believing private apparitions or miracles, the Church advises her people to use caution but to be open-minded. A particular experience or phenomenon may be believed by the faithful as credible or plausible according to human reason and human faith. Any individual may choose to believe or not believe according to his or her own heart and conscience, but only after one spends time praying, reflecting upon and studying Scripture/pronouncements of the Church.

To prematurely disregard the authenticity of any supernatural experience without following the above criteria is to show irrational judgment, narrow-mindedness, and perhaps, even disobedience to the teachings of the Church. It is also wrong to believe these occurrences immediately without discernment and reflection. Both extremes may discredit the authentic works of God in our midst, or play host to sensational and emotional displays of imagination.

Throughout history God has intervened in extraordinary ways in the lives of favored souls, people of every denomination. In the Catholic Church alone there are hundreds of documented cases on record of various saints and mystics who have had supernatural experiences from the time of Jesus Christ to the present day.

Over the years, it is St. Therese of Lisieux (The Little Flower), St. Francis of Assisi and St. Theresa of Avila who have most frequently appeared to favored souls. Some modern day saints who have performed miracles for those requesting their intercession include, Padre Pio, the Italian

---

*This group also includes deceased family members who are in Heaven.

stigmatist; Sister Elizabeth Ann Seton and St. John Neumann, America's first native-born and America's first male to be cannonized; Kateri Tekakwitha, the first American Indian to be beatified; St. John Bosco, who believed that going through the Blessed Virgin Mary was the shortest way to God; Fr. Solanus Casey who has been credited with over 6000 healings, and Blessed Faustina Kowalska who received the Message of Mercy from the Lord and spent her life spreading it.

Mother Frances Cabrini was credited with healing the eyes and face of a newborn infant who was given two drops of fifty percent silver nitrate solution (instead of the usual one percent) in his eyes at birth by mistake. St. Jude and St. Joseph, while not being modern-day, continue to be popular saints for intercessions.

How can we possibly ignore such tremendous evidence that there are miracles among us? What about the thousands upon thousands reported by average people everyday? Undoubtedly, such things are happening in your own neighborhood, even in your own homes. Actually, each one of us is a living, breathing and walking miracle. From the moment of our conception when God's fingertip first touched sperm to egg, changes took place in a single cell that began to grow into a new little person. Suddenly, there was life! There was a miracle.

Of course, there will always be skeptics when it comes to the spiritual plane. Skepticism is part of human nature. We are trained to question, not only things that which pertains to the supernatural, but anything that makes us uncomfortable and intrudes into our human existence. But how can someone judge what he has not seen, known or experienced?

Surely, all the miracles that happen daily cannot be explained away as figments of over-active imaginations. There are just too many cases reported throughout history to deny the probability, reality and existence of spiritual occurrences.

Every story appearing in *The Miracle Makers* is true. Each incident has been re-created by normal, everyday good people, just like you and me, who are totally convinced that miracles are meant, not only for the benefit of one person, but that every miracle belongs to the world to lift us up, to inspire us, to amaze us and to let every man, woman and child know that God loves us and is presently working in our lives.

Because this is not a theology book, but rather, a means of giving thanks and praise to The Miracle Makers, we invite each of you to become one with us as we witness, not only what God has done for us, but what He and the Heavenly Hosts will do for those who are willing to open heart and mind for that step in faith, that confident assurance concerning what we hope for, and the conviction about things we do not see.

Introduction

For many years, the Lord has been writing plots for the stories found in this book. Now, with the help of the Holy Spirit, each re-creation becomes a work of love, all done in the name of Jesus and Mary, for the enjoyment, encouragement and enrichment of the readers—God's wonderful people who are as much, or more, deserving of His special favors as any of us who are about to offer our stories up to the Lord.

Come now! Join the Celebration.

~ CHAPTER 1 ~

The Beginning
(Tim's Story)

(Joan Wester Anderson,who first published this story of her son's rescue in her New York Times best-seller, *Where Angels Walk,* and whose newest work, *Where Wonders Prevail,* is now on bookshelves, has joined us in praising and thanking God for His intervention. Joan's writing career began in 1973. She has authored and co-authored many best-selling books and, in 1979, she launched a public-speaking career which currently takes her around the country to speak of angels and miracles. The Andersons are parents of five grown children.)

It was just past midnight on December 24, 1983. The Midwest was shivering through a record-breaking cold spell, complete with gale force winds and frozen water pipes. And although our suburban Chicago household was filled with the snug sounds of a family at rest, I couldn't be a part of them, not until our twenty-one-year-old son pulled into the driveway. At that moment, Tim and his two roommates were driving home for Christmas, their first trip back since they moved East last May. "Don't worry, Mom," Tim had reassured me over the phone last night, "We're going to leave before dawn tomorrow and drive straight through. We'll be fine!"

Kids. They do insane things. Under normal circumstances, I figured a Connecticut-to-Illinois trek ought to take about eighteen hours. But the weather had turned so dangerously cold that radio reports warned against venturing outdoors, even for a few moments. And we had heard nothing

---

from the travelers. Distressed, I pictured them on a desolate road. What if they ran into car problems or lost their way? And if they had been delayed, why hadn't Tim phoned?

Restlessly, I paced and prayed with the familiar shorthand all mothers know: God, send someone to help them.

By now, as I later learned, the trio had stopped briefly in Fort Wayne, Indiana to deposit Don at his family home. Common sense suggested that Tim and Jim stay the rest of the night and resume their trek in the morning. But when does common sense prevail with invincible young adults? There were only four driving hours left to reach home. And although it was the coldest night in Midwest history and the highways were snowy and deserted, the two had started out again.

They had been traveling for only a few miles on a rural access road to the Indiana tollway, when they noticed that the car's engine seemed sluggish, lurching erratically and dying to ten to fifteen miles per hour. Tim glanced uneasily at Jim. "Do not—" the radio announcer intoned, "—repeat, do not venture outside tonight, friends. There's a record windchill of eighty below zero, which means that exposed skin will freeze in less than a minute." The car surged suddenly, then coughed and slowed again.

"Tim," Jim spoke into the darkness, "we're not going to stall here, are we?"

"We can't," Tim answered grimly as he pumped the accelerator. "We'd die for sure."

But instead of picking up speed, the engine sputtered, chugging and slowing again. About a mile later, at the top of a small incline, the car crawled to a frozen stop.

Horrified, Tim and Jim looked at each other in the darkened interior. They could see across the fields in every direction, but, incredibly, theirs was the only vehicle in view. For the first time, they faced the fact that they were in enormous danger. There was no traffic, no refuge ahead, not even a farmhouse light blinking in the distance. It was as if they had landed on an alien, snow-covered planet.

And the appalling, unbelievable cold! Never in Tim's life had he experienced anything so intense. They couldn't run for help; he knew that for sure. He and Jim were young and strong, but even if shelter was only a short distance away, they couldn't survive. The temperature would kill them in a matter of minutes.

"Someone will come along soon," Jim muttered, looking in every direction. "They're bound to."

"I don't think so," Tim said. "You heard the radio. Everyone in the world is inside tonight—except us."

"Then what are we going to do?"

"I don't know." Tim tried starting the engine again, but the ignition key clicked hopelessly in the silence. Bone-chilling cold had penetrated the car's interior, and his feet were already growing numb. Well, God, he prayed, echoing my own distant plea. You're the only one who can help us now.

It seemed impossible to stay awake much longer . . . Then, as if they had already slipped into a dream, they saw headlights flashing at the car's left rear. But that was impossible. For they had seen no twin pinpricks of light in the distance, no hopeful approach. Where had the vehicle come from? Had they already died?

But no. For, miraculously, someone was knocking on the driver's side window. "Need to be pulled?" In disbelief they heard the muffled shout. But it was true. Their rescuer was driving a tow truck.

"Yes! Oh, yes, thanks!" Quickly, the two conferred as the driver, saying nothing more, drove around to the front of the car and attached chains. If there were no garages open at this hour, they would ask him to take them back to Don's house, where they could spend the rest of the night.

Swathed almost completely in a furry parka, hood and a scarf up to his eyes, the driver nodded at their request but said nothing more. He was calm, they noted as he climbed into his truck, seemingly unconcerned about the life-threatening circumstances in which he had found them. Strange that he's not curious about us, Tim mused, and isn't even explaining where he came from or how he managed to approach without our seeing him . . . And had there been lettering on the side of the truck? Tim hadn't noticed any. He's going to give us a big bill, on a night like this. I'll have to borrow some money from Don or his dad . . . But Tim was exhausted from the ordeal, and gradually, as he leaned against the seat, his thoughts slipped away.

They passed two locked service stations, stopped to alert Don from a pay phone, and were soon being towed back through the familiar Fort Wayne neighborhood. Hushed, Christmas lights long since extinguished and families asleep, Don's still seemed the most welcoming street they had ever been on. The driver maneuvered carefully around the cul-de-sac and pulled up in front of Don's house. Numb with cold, Tim and Jim raced to the side door where Don was waiting, then tumbled into the blessedly warm kitchen, safe at last.

Don slammed the door against the icy blast. "Hey, what happened?" he began, but Tim interrupted.

"The tow truck driver, Don—I have to pay him. I need to borrow" he began.

"Wait a minute." Don frowned, looking past his friends through the window. "I don't see any tow truck out there."

Tim and Jim turned around. There, parked alone at the curb, was Tim's car. There had been no sound in the crystal-clear night of its release from the chains, no door slam, no chug of an engine pulling away. There had been no bill for Tim to pay, no receipt to sign, no farewell or "thank you" or "Merry Christmas." Stunned, Tim raced back down the driveway to the curb, but there were no taillights disappearing in the distance, no engine noise echoing through the silent streets, nothing at all to mark the tow truck's presence.

Then Tim saw the tire tracks traced in the windblown snowdrifts. But there was only one set of marks ringing the cul-de-sac curve. And they belonged to Tim's car . . .

Was it an angel? Our family will never know for sure.

But on Christmas Eve in 1983, I heard the whisper of wings as a tow-truck driver answered a heavenly summons and brought our son safely home.

When Christmas carols fill the air and our worries regress in a temporary whirl of holiday nostalgia, everyone believes in angels. But it's harder to accept the likelihood that the "multitude of heavenly hosts" on that long-ago Bethlehem hillside has relevance in our lives, too; that God's promise to send His angels to protect and rescue each of His children is a faithful pact, continuing for all eternity, throughout every season of the year.

Angels don't get much attention today. If the spirit world is acknowledged at all, it's usually the dark side, the bizarre satanic cults that are wreaking so much havoc, especially among our youth. Yet there is evidence that good spirits are also at work here on earth, combating evil, bringing good news, warning us of danger, consoling us in our suffering . . . then vanishing, just as the angels did on that first Christmas night.

Angels don't submit to litmus tests, testify in court, or slide under a microscope for examination. Thus, their existence cannot be "proved" by the guidelines we humans usually use.To know one, perhaps, requires a willingness to suspend judgment, to open ourselves to possibilities we've only dreamed about. "The best and most beautiful things in the world cannot be seen or even touched," Helen Keller said. "They must be felt with the heart."

(For information regarding angels in assumed bodies, refer to Chapter 13, pages 1 & 2)

~ CHAPTER 2 ~

Miracles and Messengers of Faith

> "The very presence of an angel is a communication. Even when an angel crosses our path in silence, God has said to us, 'I am here. I am present in your life.'"
>
> Tobias Palmer, AN ANGEL IN MY HOUSE

Whenever God detects our special needs or hears an urgent prayer, He summons his powerful winged messengers to his side, gives each a particular assignment and sends them on their way.

Instantly, there is a rustle of angels—soft, slight sounds, whispers, gentle stirrings of wind, feathers rubbing, unruffled, one against the other. Silent sounds, giggles, unseen even by the breeze as heavenly beings diligently go about, fulfilling their Master's wishes.

Every moment of every day these miraculous ventures take place just beyond the curtain that divides the reality of Heaven and Earth. This is the realm of the Divine Dimension, that space in which miracles happen, and into which those blessed with spiritual sensitivity are allowed to peek each time an angelic or Marian (that of the Blessed Mother) intervention occurs. Whether entry to this world of wonder is gained strictly through the living of a good life and prayer is not completely understood. However, logic and experience should tell us that those who pray and really get to know Our Lord, the Blessed Virgin, the angels and the saints are more likely to see that threshold than those who ignore their heavenly hosts.

For those who find belief in the spiritual difficult to accept, we would ask you to try this: Close your eyes. Imagine yourself at a time in your life when you were at your lowest point—a time when you faced real danger, or a time that some insurmountable problem threatened you or someone dear to you. Now, suppose something totally unexpected and miraculous happened that saved you from the situation. Could you then believe in miracles, or, at least, acknowledge that a Blessed Coincidence had taken place?

> *BLESSED COINCIDENCE:* A mini-miracle God performs behind our backs to shield us, support us or simply surround us with His love!

Let me give you an example: In December 1995 when my husband Larry and I headed west toward Denver via Route 36, it was a quieter highway that ran through and passed many friendly but smaller Midwestern towns.

Thursday evening we stayed in Maryville, Kansas. The next morning we were on the road again, just as the sun was climbing above the eastern horizon.

Larry asked me if we might find a First Friday Mass.

"That could be difficult here in the middle of Kansas," I replied. But before I could even swallow, we noticed a green road sign straight ahead: **MANKATO 5**

"Great!" I said. "What time is it?"

"It's 7:55. Let's see if there's an eight o'clock Mass here," Larry replied.

Five minutes later, after following directions we received at a service station, we entered St. Theresa's Church just as the 8 o'clock Communion Service was beginning. The Eucharistic Minister standing behind the altar and three people who were kneeling in the front pew, looked around and smiled at the sound of footsteps. Then, the service continued.

Afterwards, we told them of the coincidental relationship between the miles to Mankato and the time, plus our walking into the service just as it was beginning. Then, we drove on toward Denver.

By Sunday afternoon, our visit with my Aunt Marguerite was completed, and we started driving home on Route 36. After spending the night in Norton, Kansas we found ourselves basking in Monday's first rays of sunlight as, cruising at the speed limit, we rehashed the trip. I was behind the wheel and in no particular hurry when Larry asked again about finding a Mass.

"Here in the middle of Kansas!" I remarked, never imagining we would be as fortunate as three days earlier. Then, straight ahead of us there was a green road sign that read: **MANKATO 5**

I was speechless. But Larry quickly held his arm so that I could see the face of his watch. "It's five minutes to eight again!" he said, the tone of his voice reflecting my amazement and disbelief.

This time our Buick LeSabre almost found its way to St. Theresa's Church. The Communion service was starting, as it had been on the previous Friday.

The same Eucharistic Minister at the altar, and his wife in the front row, looked dumbfounded at seeing us again. They couldn't have been anymore surprised than we were at the Blessed Coincidence that had taken place, the mini-miracle that God performed behind our backs to, as in this case, support us and simply surround us with His love.

Afterwards we joined the Eucharistic Minister and his wife, Bill and Loretta Kimminau, for coffee and discussed what the odds must be on being at the exact spot and time, twice, on an eight-hundred mile trip, with no prior planning. The Lord had gained our attention. We wondered what He had in mind.

As it turned out, it was Bill who sent us the Rosary tape that I was praying on behalf of our grandbaby, only hours before something special happened. (See "Anna's Frame"–Chapter 3)

It is because of miracles, interventions and Blessed Coincidences, such as this, that we now **BOAST ONLY OF WHAT GOD HAS DONE!** In 1 Cor.1:31 Paul says, **"Let him who would boast, boast in the Lord!"**

"If you want your neighbor to know what the Lord will do for him, let him see and hear what He has done for you." (Lee McLellan, QUIPS, QUOTES AND QUESTS)

By sharing these very personal stories, we hope to increase awareness of the many miraculous things that already have been, could be, or will be happening in your life or in the lives of those you love. Because God's way and His timing is so unpredictable by our standards, there is no way to forecast what may happen in the future. All we can do is make only wise decisions as we move along the difficult path of choices toward Heaven, and make the Miracle Makers our dearest friends and allies. Then, somewhere along the way, something miraculous could happen, and when it does, you WILL believe in miracles.

When Jesus walked our earth, He thought of us and said, "Blest are they who have not seen, and have believed." (John 20:29)

We are all God's children and heirs of Heaven. The Lord loves us all equally, unconditionally and without exception, and He is as close to one of us as he is another. Still, man often chooses to ignore Him, even when there are beautiful miracles just waiting to happen around the corner of any fervent prayer.

Prayer? Yes, prayer, that dialogue between God and man. The Almighty only asks that we pray and obey his Commandments. You will notice how the powerful pair of patience and prayer intertwines and threads itself through the stories in this book. It binds them together.

One such sampler of God's handiwork and faith comes in the form of Julia, a delightful eighty-some-year-old lady who spoke of prayer and what it has done for her. In the 1970's when an X-ray revealed a spot on her lung, not only did she pray, she asked the priest to lay hands on her for healing. A few days later, a second X-ray was spot free.

Another time, as Julia walked to church, she slipped and fell backwards on the ice. X-rays revealed the presence of arthritis in her back, a condition of which she had been totally unaware. Soon Julia developed stiffness and pain in her joints, until she had to use a cane and walker. One night, she prayed fervently for healing and with the dawn came freedom from the arthritic misery that has never returned.

Then, recently, Julia underwent serious surgery and recovery for cancer. She feels strongly that it was, not only her prayers, but the prayers of others that healed her once again.

As with Julia's prayers, ours should fit us like an old shoe, comfortably, and conforming to each one's upbringing and beliefs. We may wish to read, chant or say our favorite prayers or devotions (rosaries, novenas, Scripture), or we may simply prefer to TALK to Jesus and Mary as we go about our daily activities. Others repeat the name of "Jesus! Jesus! Jesus!" as a short but power-filled prayer that can be said many times a day. It's not so much a matter of what you say as making sure you take out the time TO PRAY! (For those wishing to take their prayer life to a higher plane, refer to Ella Marie Reiter's "Mary At My Window Watching" in Chapter 6. There she humbly details her spiritual growth, done through Our Lady's guidance.)

Since noise is distracting, find a quiet spot in which to read, pray and meditate. Then, listen for God's reply! Let Him speak to the inner you. And once He or the Blessed Mother grants a request, don't forget to THANK THEM!

1. Remember that: "There are only two times to praise God, when you feel like it and when you don't!"
Even Albert Einstein said, "There are only two ways to live your life. One, as if NOTHING is a miracle. The other, as if EVERYTHING is a miracle." (Which way sounds like the most fun?)

Would you recognize a miracle? After speaking with many people who have experienced one, and having been blessed myself, the agreement is that, "There's no mistaking a miracle for anything else!" The moment that spiritual something happens, you know it! You are overcome with unexplainable awe, wonder, joy and a disbelief that quickly gives way to sheer delight, and a feeling of total unworthiness. Side effects include: chills, tingles, weak knees and lots of tears.

And you will never, ever forget the incident. Afterwards, praying becomes, not only a privilege, but a way of life as you try to please God in any way you can.

In Dan Wakefield's book *Expect a Miracle,* he quoted Fr. Gerald O'Rourke as saying, "We never acknowledge miracles. We're stingy; we don't share our miracles and they die on us. How blessed we are, but there's no acknowledgment of it, we never mention it. If we don't speak of it, we diminish the possibility of miracles."

However, some interventions are so private and personal, they cannot possibly be shared. We understand that, and for those who cherish these events in their hearts, as well as readers who feel they have nothing to relate, we have a surprise for you. Everyone can become part of this book.

Chapter 14 belongs to you! "Between God and Me" has been left blank so you can either : 1) Inscribe your own personal miraculous story or 2) List all the blessings in your life for which you wish to praise and thank God. (By writing and re-writing details on scrap paper first, it will make for neater entry into the book)

God, along with his messengers (the Blessed Virgin Mary and the angels) perform miraculously every day of the year. Mary still appears at Medjugorje and lesser-known places, just as she did at Guadalupe, Lourdes, Fatima, Garabandal, La Salette and others. She continues to stress prayer, conversion, fasting and penance. Her prayer of choice is the rosary, the single most powerful weapon by which the world will be won for Jesus Christ. No! This beautiful string of beads is not obsolete, as some have come to believe. It is still in vogue and performs beautifully when placed in the hands of all who are willing to use it.

In stressing penance, the Lord does not ask us to wear hair shirts or walk through flames. Instead, He asks something almost as difficult, but doable. Realizing the weakness of human nature and the difficulties of everyday life, he challenged us when He spoke to Lucia in the chapel at midnight and told her, "The sacrifice required of every person is the fulfillment of his duties in life and observance of My law. This is the penance that I now seek and require."

So, for the sake of happiness and the promise of world peace, can't we all work together on this and . . .

Praise God! Praise Mary!

~ CHAPTER 3 ~

Weapons of Silver and Gold

"For the peace of the world . . . the daily recitation of the Rosary is a necessity," Jesus told holy Marguerite of Belgium in 1966.

HOUSE CALL

by
Bill and Loretta Kimminau
(As told by Bill)

It was Easter 1996 and my wife Loretta and I were about to say the rosary. I noticed that one of the links had broken.

"After we pray, I'll put it back together," I said as I fingered the normally circular array of beads that now hung as one long chain.

But when I first tried to repair the intricate piece, I discovered that I would have to get some additional tools.

As soon as our evening meal was over, I gathered everything I needed and reached for my broken rosary.

To my amazement and delight, I realized that the chain of beads was perfectly connected at the point where it had been disconnected only a few hours earlier. No one, other than our daughter-in-law, had been in the house with us during the day, and she assured us that she hadn't touched the rosary.

Had a very special "repairman" made His skillful presence known that day? Had he made a house call at our home? What do you think?

A RING AROUND OUR ROSARIES

by
Barbara and Duke Curran
(As told by Barb)

In the spring of 1992 Duke and I, along with a bus load of people, boarded the tour bus after 8 o'clock Mass. Our pastor, still wearing his vestments, came out to bless us as we were about to pull away. I was so pleased.

We were going to the campus of Notre Dame University at South Bend, Indiana for the Medjugorjean Conference. Three visionaries from the Yugoslavian (Bosnian) Shrine were slated to give personal accounts of their lives and the visions of the Blessed Virgin Mary.

Once we were safely delivered to the campus, we became immersed in the religious event. I especially remember Ivan, one of the seers, who surprised the group with news that the Virgin Mary had appeared to him the previous night, right there on the ground on which we stood. Instantly, I felt as if the Blessed Mother had somehow touched me, as did just about everyone who was in attendance.

"And she sends her special blessings to each of you at this Conference," the friendly seer announced. Everyone who heard Ivan's words was thrilled and later, we all agreed that this had been a powerful weekend.

A few days later after we returned home, Duke and I visited with some of those who had gone with us to South Bend. It was after Mass in the vestibule. I remember looking at my rosaries and saying, "Mine haven't turned gold." Actually, it never occurred to me that they would.

But a week or so later, while I was in the Perpetual Adoration Chapel, I removed my wooden-beaded silver-linked rosary from its leather case. I couldn't believe my eyes! The silver chain had turned golden.

For a long time, chills raced through every part of my body. I realized immediately what God and his Blessed Mother had done for me, and I'll never forget that moment!

An hour later, I was excitedly telling Duke what had happened. But, was I surprised, when my husband had great news of his own.

Before we left for the Conference, he had taken his grandmother's silver rosary to the jewelers to have its crucifix repaired.

"Just awhile ago, Barb," Duke told me, "I went to the store to get my rosary. As soon as I came home and took it from the envelope, I was shocked. The crucifix on Grandma's rosary was gold. I hurried back to the jewelers, but they assured me they had done nothing to affect such a change."

Then, as we stood there, staring down at both our religious articles, we knew Our Blessed Mother had graciously placed A Golden Ring Around Our Rosaries.

Praise you, Mary and Jesus!

MARY'S GOLD

(The Heavenly Matchmaker)

by

Virginia Drew

Of course, I had heard of Medjugorje. After all, I had two brothers who went there four years earlier. But when my daughter, Peggy phoned me from Kansas City in the spring of 1989 all excited, saying, "Let's you, me and Dad go to Medjugorje in September," I was like, "Sure, BUT . . . " not really putting too much thought into it. I did mention it to my husband but he said I should go if I wanted—he wouldn't. He didn't need to trot half way around the world to see the Blessed Mother appearing; he could find her right here in Quincy, Illinois.

Wayne Weible had talked at Peggy's church about Medjugorje. He wasn't even Catholic at the time but he had such convincing convictions that she was anxious to go. She was single, but I was dragging my feet because I had two kids in grade school, one in high school and another in college. I couldn't go without feeling guilty.

One evening in late May I sneaked away from the noise of the TV, kids, etc. to my bedroom to say my rosary. As I knelt at the side of my bed in the dark, the phone rang. I had just begun praying. Then, someone yelled, "Mom, Peg's on the line!"

I got to my feet, laid the rosary down on the desk, turned on the light, picked up the phone and proceeded to talk with my daughter. Of course, Peggy got right to the point, "Have you made a decision about going?"

I started to evade the question when I noticed rays of glimmering light radiating from my rosary. I couldn't believe my eyes! Goosebumps raised on my arms and, at first, I was unable to speak. Finally I tried to explain what was happening to Peggy. I blinked several times and, carefully, picked up the pile of beads. My rosary's links that had been silver only seconds before had been suddenly transformed to gold.

When I told Peggy, she squealed along with me. We knew that the Blessed Virgin was sending us a powerful sign that I was to go to Medjugorje. So, I went!

I didn't experience the sun dancing there, but just seeing the expressions on the faces of the Croation people as they knelt at Mass after a hard days' work, the devotion in their eyes, the way they knelt without shifting from one knee to the other, and their beautiful singing of the Ava Maria gave me real encouragement to live my faith to a higher degree. The time I spent there in private prayer and reciting the rosary with others as we journeyed up Apparition Hill or Mount Krizevac, and the trips we made through grape fields on our way to St. James for Mass was miraculous enough for me.

But what a rude awakening when, after days of such peace, we arrived back at Kennedy Airport in New York. There, the abusive language and people's lack of consideration only reinforced in me the need to spread Our Lady's message of world peace.

Oh, yes! Peggy wanted to see the sun dance. On the last day there she looked at it so hard that she ended up seeing spots before her eyes. When she returned to Kansas City, she made an appointment with an optometrist whose name she found listed in the phone book.

Her spots? Oh, they disappeared without damage to her eyes.

Her optometrist? Well, one year later—she married him!

Whenever we look for and listen to heavenly signs, we are led down paths of true wonder.

JOB'S-TEARS

(The Story of Sharon Seuferer's Love of Rosaries)

As written by
Carol Oliver

Sharon grew up in a Catholic home, attended Mass regularly and received instruction in the church. At the time of her first communion she received a gift that would be the beginning of a life-long interest in rosaries. A family friend, Uncle Billy, gave Sharon the mother-of-pearl rosary he had received at his first communion. It became her treasure.

Later, a friend Sister Cecilia, at the time of the golden anniversary of her novitiate, gave Sharon the rosary she had been given when she entered the convent. Sharon wanted to do something special in return. She carved walnut beads, snipped the barbs from fishhooks and used the shanks to connect the beads, centers, and cross. She mailed the rosary to Sister Cecilia, who was so taken with the gift that she sent Sharon a box of beads, wires, centers, and crosses gathered from her friends at the convent. With those supplies Sharon made more rosaries that were sent to India and distributed in the mission field. Sharon received a letter of gratitude.

Sister Cecilia and her friends and acquaintances began asking Sharon to make rosaries of all kinds—wooden beads, mother-of-pearl beads, glass beads, silver and gold beads, ceramic beads and Job's-tear beads, which became one of her most requested rosaries.

Sharon learned about the Job's-tear plant that produced seeds with a natural hole through the center. She ordered a package of seeds from a nursery, planted them, and nearly howed them out of the garden when they emerged long after being planted as something totally unrecognized. Sharon harvested the beads and watched them turn their characteristic beautiful gray as they dried and then discovered the thin membrane on one end that hides the hole through the center of the tear-shaped bead.

Sharon has made many, many rosaries, though she no longer cuts up fish hooks. She orders supplies (beads, centers, crosses, and wire) from a supply house and makes each rosary an original work. She is asked to set up displays of her creations at churches and receives letters and calls from around the country as people of faith wish to have certain kinds of rosaries for their own use or to give as a gift. To Sharon each rosary is a spiritual connection between maker and recipient, another connection between Sharon and God, an outgrowth of her faith.

One rosary in particular holds an unequaled place in Sharon's life. One night she awoke with a vision of a large rosary that she would hand carve from a single piece of redwood 2 by 6 inches by 13 feet. She used all of her spare minutes for weeks to complete the piece. The finished product was varnished and has thrilled many who have seen it. Its home is in a duffel bag, carried from place to place, so that the carving can be shared with any who want to see it. One day, Sharon hopes it can be blessed by the Pope.

ANNA'S FRAME

by
Mary Talken

It was almost Christmas 1995, and outside the landscape glistened while carols from the CD filled our home. Tree lights and glitter shimmered white and gold and reflected brightly off the holiday gifts stacked beneath the pine.

Around noon on December 23rd the phone rang. Our son Dan was calling from California with unsettling news—his wife Christine, who was not even six months pregnant with their second child, had been put to bed after experiencing premature contractions as close as two minutes apart.

"It's too soon, Dad," Dan told Larry. "Too soon!"

Since the obvious thing to do was to pray, we placed a prayer card in our parish's Perpetual Adoration Chapel, and then I mailed a Mass petition card to the Oblate Father's Grotto of Our Lady of Lourdes shrine in San Antonio, Texas. Ironically, my youngest daughter and I had already planned to visit the city in February. Now I had a special reason for going to the Grotto. (Read about this visit in Chapter 13)

For several days, Christine's contractions continued, despite the medication and bed rest. As hard as we prayed, asking Jesus to help soon gave way to pleading for our newest grandbaby's survival. If only God could give us a sign!

FRIDAY, DECEMBER 29th—Early that morning I turned on the Rosary Tape that had been sent to us by the couple in Mankato, Kansas. While seated in my favorite chair and with tears in my eyes, I prayed the most fervent rosary of my life for the baby. Moments later, as I walked through the living room, I thought about the silver-plated framed photo album that Larry had received as a gift at his retirement party. Because it didn't match the brass accessories in our home, I kept it underneath the end table. Oh, I might put some photos in it. I'd better get it out, I thought as I carried it to the kitchen table and placed it on the far side of the disheveled pile of old photos. I was putting them into new albums.

All morning I prayed and rearranged photographs; the baby was never out of my mind. Then, it was time for lunch. I headed for the refrigerator, and as I passed the small orphan album, I glanced down. My feet stopped moving.

What? I wondered as I stared at Larry's retirement gift. "Oh, my! Oh, my!" I repeated, over and over and over, but my eyes were having a difficult time accepting what they were seeing—the silver-plated frame on the album had turned to a golden color. Slowly I began to realize that, perhaps, a miracle had taken place in my kitchen.

My knees became wobbly. Part of me wanted to reach out to touch the frame, but I hesitated, fearing that I might somehow cause it to revert to its original silver. Tears were quickly interfering with my vision.

Then I realized this was God's way of letting me know that our grandbaby was going to be all right. Immediately, I was overcome with feelings of awe, wonder, relief, thanksgiving and total unworthiness that such a powerful thing should have happened for me. Without thinking, I grabbed the album and clutched it to my heart.

Because Larry wasn't coming home for several hours, I called my daughter Denise to share the amazing news with her. She verified that the frame had, indeed, been silver, so I phoned Dan to tell him what happened. I'm sure he was thinking, Ol' Mom's losing it! when I babbled, "The baby's going to be fine!"

Christine remained in bed with contractions for most of her remaining pregnancy, but three months later on April 3, 1996 (four days beyond her due date), Anna Elise was born, a perfect and healthy baby. Praise God!

Someday, when I no longer need my golden treasure, it will be Anna's Frame. (Pictured on cover)

Through a special note of heartfelt thanks that we put in the Adoration Chapel, we relayed our appreciation for all the intercessory prayers that ascended to the Lord. I realized that with such a treasured gift comes a responsibility, and after having asked God for several months, "Is there another book you want from me, Jesus?", I sensed that He was giving me the answer—a book pertaining to miraculous happenings in the lives of everyday people.

Other than my daughter Denise, four other people have verified that the album's frame was silver when Larry received it at his retirement party, including the gentleman who gave it to him. Praise the Miracle Makers!

~ CHAPTER 4 ~

Voices From Within

How often haven't we heard ourselves say, "Gosh, I don't know what it was, but something seemed to be telling me to . . . !"

Whether that inner voice was giving us a suggestion or a warning, whether it was daytime or nighttime, we have all experienced the feeling that we should do some particular thing, or that we should not! And how many times, after the fact, haven't you wished that you had listened when you hadn't?

The following stories present a variety of these voices, urges, instincts, warnings and sudden inspirations that were heeded. As you read them, try to recall similar incidents, or Blessed Coincidences, that happened in your own life when you listened to and followed the directions that your heart and mind heard. Who do you suppose was speaking?

NIGHT CALL

by
Billie Brod

In February of 1986 I suffered a stroke. Because of the barrage of tests I had already undergone, I was tired of doctoring, and when the time came for my yearly OB visit, I procrastinated in making an appointment.

One night I was awakened from the middle of a deep sleep. A voice inside me said, quite emphatically, "You have cancer!"

The voice was so real, so loud and frightening that I actually jumped out of the bed, which jostled and woke my husband on the other side. "What's wrong?" he stammered.

For a time, we discussed the nocturnal warning, but the importance of the message was something we both sensed. Bob insisted that I make an appointment as soon as possible.

Usually I would have to wait two months to get in to see my gynecologist. But when I phoned the following day, the nurse told me I was in luck. "Someone just canceled," she said.

The coincidence convinced me that the voice was more than a figment of my imagination. The following day I went to the Clinic for a Papp test. When the report came in the mail it indicated perfectly normal results.

Still concerned, I called the doctor and told him of my dream, the voice telling me I had cancer. Immediately, he ordered an endometrial biopsy.

This time, my fear was confirmed. I had cancer! And it had been there for a time.

Five days later, when surgery was performed, they discovered that none of the uterus' lining had been breached, even though one spot had come dangerously close to perforation, perhaps as close as a matter of days.

What can one say, think or do, but thank a caring God for his goodness and his timely NIGHT CALL, as loud as it was!

DIAMOND IN THE ROUGH

by

Mary Talken

It was a mild spring day when I first declared war on crab grass. For several hours, with knife in hand, I crawled around our backyard, frantically cutting and pulling out invading clumps of the weed. No gloves. Just me, barehanded, against the enemy.

That evening I prepared dinner and did a few chores around the house. The next morning, after having my hair styled, I shopped for groceries and returned home to vacuum, clean and cook.

Just before dinner, the empty prongs of my wedding ring scratched me. "Larry!" I cried. "My diamond's gone. My beautiful diamond!"

My husband of thirty-eight years was very sympathetic. "Don't worry, honey. I'll get you another one."

"But I don't want another one," I pouted like a spoiled child. "I want the one you gave me at our wedding."

Quickly, I tried to recount everything I had done over the past two days. The yard, the stores, the shag carpets I'd vacuumed, the car and the city streets. I'll never find it! I decided. Besides a tiny one-quarter caret clear stone would be terribly transparent in such a big cluttered-up world. That night I cried and prayed to God, Mary, the angels and every saint I could think of. At bedtime, I was wide awake, but finally, I sensed that God would help me and fell asleep.

At 5:30 a.m., after returning to my bed from a trip to the bathroom, I lay in the dimness of the room, thinking. Suddenly, a thought came to mind. I should get up and walk around the house, barefooted. Maybe I would feel something with my toes.

In the soft glow of night lights, I moved slowly around the bed, passed our dresser and into the hall where our walk-in closet lay just opposite the bathroom Larry and I had entered and exited many times over the past few days. Perhaps if I directed all my sensitivity to my feet, I'd find something, I thought, as I wiggled my toes in the pile. But there was . . .

Nothing! Tears came to my eyes.

"Help me, Jesus. PLEASE!" I begged in the semi-darkness. "Please!"

By now, I was standing in the center of the closet. Suddenly, I sensed that I should head for the same bathroom from which I had just come. As I moved toward the doorway, my instincts told me to stop, turn on the bathroom light and look down.

As my vision adjusted to the sudden brightness, I glanced at the floor and noticed that something was lying there, just in front of the tip of my right big toe. A glint! A sparkle! Something was glittering and sitting there, buoyed up on tips of blue carpet fiber, as if laughing and saying, "Here I am. Come, get me!"

"Larry! Larry!" I cried as I bent over to retrieve the tiny clear stone, careful not to lose it in the pile. "I found my diamond. I found it."

From around the corner where he was still in bed, my husband's sleepy voice trailed, "Great! I just asked St. Joseph."

WAS THAT YOU CALLING, LORD?

by
Betty Geisendorfer

As an infant, my body's rejection of milk almost led to my death until my father discovered that fresh milk drawn from cows would stay down. Then, at the age of five, I developed double pneumonia and was admitted to St. Mary's Hospital. My parents were Baptists; still, they enjoyed watching the Franciscan nuns sit me down among a pile of toys at the foot of the Blessed Mother's statue at the end of the hallway. I remember looking up into the beautiful glazed face of Mary, thinking of her as a mother watching over me.

When I was twelve, my older sister became a Catholic at the time of her marriage. I believe it was then that a seed of faith was planted in me as I prayed that God would lead me in the right path.

The following year at the age of thirteen, I was baptized a Baptist. It was a happy occasion for me, and as soon as we returned home, I headed for my room where I sat down in my rocker. Suddenly, I sensed an unusual sensation washing over me, quietly surrounding me and enveloping me in an aura of warmth, joy and total fulfillment. It was as if I was wrapped inside a cocoon of love!

But before long, Mother's call brought me back to the reality of my room, no matter how I fought to remain in that peace-filled moment. I wished it could stay forever, but it disappeared.

During my teens, God took a back seat in my life, even though I didn't forget Him. Still, the rumblings of desire to join the Catholic faith were there, and with each passing year, the desire became stronger.

Eventually, I met and married George. But I rarely mentioned religion because, even though he was a good person, he saw no need for church and the like.

We were blessed with three sons. When I was twenty-five and it was the Vigil of Easter, I asked God to give me a sign if He wanted me to become a Catholic.

That evening, we were invited to dine at a friend's house. This was back in the days when the Lenten Abstinence lasted until midnight on Good Saturday. The hostess had prepared a meal that included meat, so when one of the Catholic men said, "Please, everyone go ahead and eat the meat. I just can't partake until midnight," I was impressed.

At the same time George looked at me and said, "You might as well fast, too. You're going to become Catholic!"

Instantly, I felt as if I'd been hit by a comet. Here was the sign I had prayed for! My husband had no interest in religion and I'd not mentioned looking for a sign.

During the days and months that followed, not only did I take instructions for entry into the Catholic Church, but George allowed our three sons to accompany me. Within a year, the four of us were baptized Catholics.

Many untold blessings continued to fill our lives. Among them, the births of two daughters and another son. But it wasn't until recently that I learned of the depths of God's love for me.

Hypoglycemia (low blood sugar) had been a problem for many years, but only within the past five had it been diagnosed. Even though I controlled it with diet most of the time, I discovered that stress could trigger a shock attack.

At the same time, George became concerned over his own health problems. He was diagnosed with ulcers and admitted to the hospital for transfusions to replace blood loss. At first he responded well and was told he could go home in a few days. But there were complications and his white blood count skyrocketed. He was taken to surgery for exploratory examination.

After the doctors removed several inches of his colon, I became quite concerned and prayed for George's recovery. Again, everything progressed well and we were about to leave the hospital when my husband's white count went back up—the colon and stomach sutures had come apart. George underwent another surgery.

May 13, 1996—The operation was finished and George's vital signs looked good. I felt comfortable in leaving him so I could get some sleep in the ICU waiting room. I was really tired and looked forward to taking my husband home soon.

Before long I drifted off into a deep sleep. Sometime after midnight, I heard a voice saying, "Betty!"

"Betty!"

"Betty!"

The voice was softly trying to wake me. It repeated, "Betty!" Then, once more, "Betty!"

I sat straight up, certain someone was calling me about George's condition. I looked around the dimly-lit room, but there was no one in sight.

It was then I felt the considerable perspiration on my arms. In fact, my entire body seemed wet and my nose was cold. I trembled and realized that I was going into a hypoglycemic shock. No one was there to help.

Just as my mind was becoming a blur, I noticed something lying on the end table. It was yellow, ripe and beautiful, a banana left there by my daughter who understood what stress could do to me. She had helped to save my life.

My other Savior was the one who had prodded me to "wake up!" to the danger at hand.

"Was that you calling, Lord?"

Of course, it was!

Yes, someone intervened to save my life that night. Unfortunately, the following day a sudden blood clot took the life of my husband.

Of course, I miss my dear George very much, but I find great comfort in picturing him with our loving and caring God in his Heavenly home.

1. "Tears are the telescope through which men see far into Heaven."

WHISPERS OF ANGELS

by

Sharon Kay

I feel that I have always been surrounded by God's angels but only in the past few years have I known this in my heart. It was something I didn't understand when, as a child, I was told about my guardian angel.

But even before I reached the age of one, I believe my special guardian whispered a warning in my ear one night. I remember my mother telling me that she and I were seated in our living room. She was otherwise occupied while I played busily on the floor.

Apparently, something outside the window wasn't as it should have been, and an inner instinct let me know about it. I began to jabber and point, making a lot of fuss and commotion until Mom finally got up off the sofa.

She hurried toward the window. The man who had been standing just outside watching us, raced away.

My mother often credited my unusually mature action as having possibly saved us from an unpleasant experience. I attribute it to the Whispers of Angels.

SOUNDS OF A SAVIOR

by
Brian Brod

Part 1:

I have always enjoyed driving things—tricycles, bicycles, trucks, cars, motorcycles and now, I'm married and I drive the big rigs, the 18-wheelers. And as you would expect, truck drivers have their share of close encounters, two of mine dealing specifically with the spiritual kind.

I remember that hazy day one autumn when at 2:00 in the afternoon I was behind the wheel of my semi headed for Fort Dodge, Iowa. Having already driven most of the night before, I was really tired and had been feeling it. My eyes blinked, closed and my head must have bowed toward my chest. I drifted off, but for how long, I'm not sure.

Suddenly, I heard two very loud thuds and the sound of "Bang! Bang!" beating on the top of my cab's roof. Startled, I opened my eyes, blinked and wondered, Did I hit something? No! I was out in the middle of the highway, and nothing was around me anywhere. I was safe! Thanks to the Sound Of A Savior's loving but loud fist.

Part 2:

During the winter of '95-'96 I was behind the wheel of my semi again, this time enroute to Muscatine, Iowa. At some point, I noticed that there was something wrong with the trailer. (The type of trailer I pull is called an air-ride, which means that instead of riding on springs, it rides on air bags for a smoother trip.)

After pulling off the highway, I crawled underneath the trailer to inspect the damage. One of the supports near the axle had come loose, so I tried to wrap a chain around the axles to pull them together until I could reach my destination where the problem could be corrected.

At the time, I was seated on the shoulder of the road under the back part of the trailer. To either side of my head was an air bag, and each bag contained 30,000 pounds of pressure. I worked from fifteen to twenty minutes, attempting to pull the damaged axles together.

All of a sudden I heard a voice speaking to me inside my head. "Get out of here now!" it demanded. For several seconds, I just sat there thinking, That's weird!

But then I heard the voice again, even louder, insisting, "Get out of here!"

Without hesitation, I scurried from beneath the trailer, jumped to my feet and backed up about ten feet. For three to five seconds, I stood there.

Then—"KABOOM!" One of the air bags exploded, and the force knocked me backward several feet as if someone had landed a punch in my belly.

When I realized what had just transpired, I lifted my heart in thanksgiving to Heaven. There hadn't been the slightest warning from the bag, not the sound of a leak or anything. Only the Sound Of A Savior's voice that saved my life that day.

1. DON'T FORGET—IF YOUR KNEES ARE KNOCKING, KNEEL ON THEM!

~ CHAPTER 5 ~

The Power of Intercession

When children want something special from their daddies, they ask their mother to intercede for them. When mothers intuitively feel that their child is in danger, they intercede with God for their youngster's safety. This is exactly what Joan Wester Anderson did for her son Tim when he was late arriving home for Christmas vacation, and this is exactly what millions of parents do nightly while their teenagers are growing up. I'm sure there's not a mother or father who hasn't stood waiting at the window or door, his or her nose pressed against the cold glass, waiting for a teenager's car to pull into the driveway, while asking God to surround their offspring with angels.

The stories in this chapter show how prayers of intercession ultimately affect the outcome for others. Since we are all God's children and He is our Heavenly Father, we can either go directly to him with our petitions, or we can ask the Blessed Mother to intercede with her Son for us.

THE BURNING BRANCH

by
Mary Talken

Even though my husband Larry worked a regular job in town for years, he enjoyed doing things in his spare time that he liked: riding horses and farming the 23-acre field north of our house. In March 1996 he pointed to an old gnarled elm tree that grew along one edge of the barren field.

"It needs to come out!" Larry told me as he explained how the root system drew vital moisture from the crops. That afternoon, the burning process began when he touched a match to fuel oil splashed around the base of the ill-fated tree.

At first, hungry flames ate their way up the ragged trunk, licking the top branches, some quite heavy and thick. Because of its age and hard wood, the blackened elm smoldered, casting an eerie, shimmering radiance against the dark veil of night.

Every evening Larry stoked the hot spots, rekindling flames for a time. By the fourth day, as my husband was leaving the house dressed in old coveralls and a cap, I asked, "Must you go out again tonight?"

"This should be the last time," he assured me and left.

Almost an hour later at around 9:45 p.m., I remember looking up and, for some unknown reason, I said out loud in the empty room, "Jesus, please help Larry!" Even though I wondered momentarily why I had said the prayer at that point, I wasn't concerned and continued to watch my program.

Shortly after 10:30, Larry returned to the TV room, clad in his housecoat and ready to relax. The minute his head hit the back of his recliner, he drifted off to sleep.

The next morning, after we joined the Mall walkers for four brisk rounds, I mentioned the randomly-said prayer.

"You prayed for me shortly before ten?" Larry asked, a surprised look on his face.

I nodded affirmatively, almost catching my toe on a raised brick.

"I wasn't going to say anything to you, Mary, but last night something happened," Larry began as we passed several people.

"What?"

"Nothing, thank heavens! But it could have," he replied, and with that, Larry described the effect that intense gnawing heat has on obstinate wood. Even though most of the elm's smaller branches had been devoured by the flames, three large charred chunks of wood refused to fall. Instead, they hung on with every pulsating breath of molten vapor they breathed.

"I realized that one of them might collapse. Still, they seemed so stubborn," my youthful-looking husband insisted, grim-faced and serious. "But at around 9:45 last night when you say you asked Jesus to help me, I was bending over raking debris into piles. Suddenly, there was a loud 'Pop!' overhead, followed by a 'Snap!' and then, a 'Thud!' When I looked up, I froze where I stood. One of the three chunks, the one directly above me, had disappeared. Apparently, it had severed itself and, if it had fallen naturally, the log would have landed on my back, probably knocking me out and setting my clothes afire."

Larry's heart was beating so loud, I could almost hear it.

"Mary, something miraculously turned that plummeting ember enough so that it balanced and wedged itself into the only fork left on the tree." There were tears in Larry's eyes as he continued. "I could have been cremated."

With that, we grabbed onto each other's hands. There was no need for words, only silent prayers of thanksgiving.

"The angel of the LORD encamps/around those who fear him, and delivers them." (Ps. 34:8)

HEAVENLY HAWAII

by
Ed J. & Marilyn Schumer
(As told by Ed)

It had been a year or so since Connie and Bruce, a couple we met who worked for a St. Louis airline, told us they might be able to give us some of their leftover stand-by courtesy coupons for air travel. Extra tickets would come in handy for my wife Marilyn, a Hawaiian native, who enjoyed flying home to visit her family and her aging parents who still resided on the Pacific paradise.

But nothing had come of the offer so, in February 1996 when air fares took a tumble in price, my wife purchased a non-refundable ticket for a May 14th flight to the island. Despite her parents health problems, she knew they would be pleased, so she telephoned them with the news.

But the response from Eusebio and Faith was not what Marilyn had expected. Her father was suffering from pulmonary edema (congestive heart failure) and, even though his doctor wanted to admit him to a hospital in Honolulu, Eusebio opted to spend what time he had left at home.

Not only were Marilyn and I shocked by the prognosis, we were concerned because Eusebio didn't attend church, and we worried about his soul. We prayed that one day he would find his own way back to God. Now we would have to pray harder.

With a non-refundable ticket in her purse, my wife found herself in a quandary. "If I leave now and Dad lives several more months, I'll be upset," Marilyn said. "But if I put off going until May and he dies next month, I'll feel just as guilty."

That night Marilyn awoke from a sound sleep and thought, Please, Lord, give me a clear sign if I'm to go to Hawaii before May.

That Saturday after attending my step-mother's eightieth birthday party in St. Louis, we stayed overnight with my brother. We mentioned the possibility of our youngest son Lucas and me accompanying Marilyn on her Hawaiian flight.

When we returned to Perryville on Sunday, Lucas discovered an envelope tucked in the side of the frame as he opened the door. He tossed it on my chair.

When I noticed the envelope, I asked Marilyn about it. She shrugged her shoulders.

"It was in the front door," Lucas explained.

As soon as I opened the envelope and saw airline coupons, I knew Connie and Bruce had come through for us. What beautiful timing, I thought, and after counting the coupons, I discovered there were seven passes to anywhere in the United States.

Marilyn was ecstatic. "It's my sign!" she cried. "We must go to see Dad soon. Perhaps on his birthday, March 15th."

Everyone was excited about the unexpected blessing. Our benefactors had no idea how many were in our family and, certainly, could not have known about our dilemma.

Clearly, God was in control. I thanked Him, decided to turn the reins of my life over to Him, and sat back to watch what He would still do for us.

Marilyn and I telephoned our grown children. Nicole, our daughter and student at Southwestern State College, informed us that spring break would begin March 15th. She could go!

Our son Marcus who lived in Cape Girardeau and who had no vacation time left and whose job usually kept him tied down, was able to go because his boss's house had burned recently and everyone's attention had shifted to the rebuilding. His wife Michelle, like Nicole, would be on spring break and their son Tyler could fly free because he was under two.

Our daughter Dina lived in Wentzville and was free to accompany us after her husband Todd offered to get someone to work in her place at the restaurant. Granddaughter Olivia, like Tyler, was under two years of age.

Of course, Marilyn and Lucas were available, but I was a carpenter who hadn't caught up with all my business in over a year. Ironically, the big job that I expected to come through, didn't, and I was able to go. There were seven tickets for seven people. Praise God!

A few days later when Marilyn phoned her father's doctor about the availability of allergy shots for herself in Hawaii, she inquired about her father's condition.

"Not many people know this, Marilyn, but your father has liver cancer. It's bad!" the physician admitted. "He could go at anytime."

Realizing that my father-in-law needed help quickly, my prayer group interceded with God on Eusebio's behalf. We asked that the terminally-ill man be allowed to wear the blessed medals and scapulars that we would take to his bedside, the articles I had brought home with me from our trip to Medjugorje.

During those final days before the flight we prayed for Eusebio, a Filipino by birth.

Then, beginning on Monday March 11th we began calling TWA Reservations for any available standby seating to Hawaii. We assumed we would never be able to fly together, so we were willing to go as couples on different flights.

But on Monday, all planes were filled to capacity! Tuesday no room! Wednesday, filled up again! Thursday-nothing available!

Finally, on Friday, March 15th (Eusebio's birthday), the day considered busiest for an airline, there were more than enough seats available. We occupied one entire row of the airplane, all nine of us.

What we could not have known was that, while we were in the air, Marilyn's sister Gloria had telephoned our house. Their father had suffered a seizure, and after the family called 911, the paramedics were bound by their rules to transport Eusebio to the hospital, even though he wished to remain at home.

At the Honolulu airport Gloria met us with news that Marilyn's father had died a few hours earlier. Visibly distressed at being too late to help her Dad either physically or spiritually, my wife cried. Little did she know the surprise that would greet us at the hospital.

The family arranged with the staff to leave Eusebio's body in the bed in which he had died until our family could see him and say our goodbyes together.

Later, we learned that when Eusebio was wheeled into the Emergency Room the day before, a Filipino priest who just happened to be there at the time, began to speak with the dying man. An instant rapport was established, possibly because they both spoke the same dialect. The priest administered the last rites and the final confession to a man who was finally turning back to God.

Everyone who was in the area at the time said the same thing—that Eusebio was filled with all the joy and anticipation of a child going home to his birthday party, a child who was all aglow with smiles and laughter as he prepared to leave Heavenly Hawaii for Heaven. Praise God!

"Come and see the works of God,/his tremendous deeds among men." (Ps. 66:5)

SOMEBODY UP THERE LIKES YOU!

by
Peggy Phillips

It was in August of 1991 that my equilibrium became strangely affected and I began to experience dizziness. One morning, I stepped off the curb and fell to my knees.

An MRI disclosed the presence of both a tumor and swelling on the brain.

"But I feel fine!" I insisted to the dedicated physician whose response was to admit me immediately to our local hospital.

My family and friends joined me in praying. They placed a prayer card in the Perpetual Adoration Chapel where people are on their knees around-the-clock, every day of the year.

That same day I remember being quite concerned when a Franciscan Priest stopped by my room to administer the Sacrament of the Sick. At the time, I believed it to be the Last Rites and it scared me. But I'll never forget the comfort that came over me when the priest anointed me with the holy oils.

Two days later they took me to the Mayo Clinic where another MRI confirmed the lesion. Unfortunately, it was located too precariously in the brain for a biopsy, so I was told, "This could be indicative of several serious conditions."

On our way home, my balance began to return. I was happy. But when we returned to Mayo's the following week in September, a second MRI showed that the lesion was still there.

"We'll wait and see," was all the doctor could say.

Prayers continued for my healing. I was so grateful for all the concern shown for me, and after three months passed into December, I headed back to Rochester for a re-evaluation/MRI.

Later in the doctor's office, I was handed a piece of paper. "Here! Read what it says at the top!" the physician insisted.

Slowly and with hands shaking, I tried to decipher the medical jargon and terminology. Finally, I looked up.

"What it says," the doctor interpreted, "is that your tumor seems to have disappeared. Somebody up there likes you!"

In sheer relief, I sighed and reached out to give the physician a big hug.

"He sure does," I babbled. "He sure does!"

Peggy's experience is only one of thousands in which prayers of intercession have summoned the healing hands of the Great Physician. Praise the Lord!

IN TUNE WITH GOD

by
Sharon Seuferer

I was the eighth of ten children and very shy, but even as a youngster, I noticed that I had a very special relationship with God. As I finished high school and worked for my parents on their 460-acre farm, I thought about the kind of life I wanted, but the usual city-marriage-children sequence didn't seem to be for me. I turned my life over to God, knowing that He would lead me where I was to go to fulfill His will.

I was to be a farmer, where I could be outdoors, close to nature and to the Lord. I relish the renewing seasons, the cycles of birth and growth, and the continuing rediscovery of the land on which I live.

As a member of a wonderful outgoing family who worked and played hard (we often gathered for evenings of family music and good times), I learned to love music. Today it speaks to me as it did then when I learned to play the guitar, harmonica and tambourine. When I was too shy to speak, I reached out with my music and now I'm known as the One-Woman Band, a real Toe Picker, because I play four instruments at once, one with my bare feet.

While playing one guitar with my fingers, I use the brightly-painted-red big toe of my right foot to strike the strings of the guitar on the floor. By wearing a neck holder for my harmonica, I can play it with and to the beat of a tambourine that is securely fitted around my left foot's shoe. For sixteen years, I have entertained crowds at the Iowa State Fair, in churches and at other gatherings over a four-state area.

But life isn't all music and fun. Farming is dangerous! I remember that summer of 1987 when I was cutting up a tree to be used as wood for the winter's heating supply. Having handled a chain saw for many years, I had learned to have great respect for its power and potential for doing serious harm.

That day I had put in long hours and was finishing the work with a dulled saw. Things were going well, and I had just placed the tip of the saw under a branch to make an upward cut, when suddenly, the saw slipped.

The upward pull brought the implement straight up toward my head. When the buzzing chain hit the left side of my face, it clipped my eyebrow and cut through my cheek. Then, it came down to bite into my collar bone and the muscle of my left shoulder.

Fortunately for me, my father never allowed me to work alone. He rushed me into the house where my mother clapped a clean towel over my face. They drove me to a nearby doctor who took one look at me and ordered an ambulance to take me to a Des Moines hospital. The damage was so extensive they thought I would surely suffer long-term nerve damage as well as permanent disfigurement to my face.

But my sister phoned a close friend of mine, who immediately set a prayer circle in motion on my behalf.

Later, inside the ambulance, I remember telling everyone, "I'll go in this ambulance to get stitched up, but I'm entertaining in Mt. Pleasant on Friday!"

Of course, no one believed me, so they kept silent.

The doctor in Des Moines looked into my fearful eyes, covered my hand with his and said, "Let's both thank God that this wasn't worse than it is. I can fix this!"

At that moment, I relaxed, not only into his care, but into the care of God.

Amazingly, the doctor gave me permission to fulfill my engagement IF I followed his regimen of care for the wound and myself. Over the next four days, I put on thirteen performances with a large bandage covering the left side of my face. The crowd's response was overwhelming, and I felt their love coming back to me as I sang and played.

When I returned to my favorite surgeon's office on Friday morning, he was surprised at the speed of the healing process. Today my smile is full and there has been no nerve damage or facial disfigurement—a witness to the miraculous power of prayer when applied liberally to the skillful hands of a surgeon.

A HELPER THROUGH THE HAZE

by

Leona Richardet

In 1987 after my daughter Marilyn and her husband separated, they tried to reconcile, but their differences were insurmountable. She found herself aboard the merry-go-round of raising two children while taking additional college courses toward a better job and working in the bakery of a local grocery store at the same time.

When stress and everyday pressures resulted in severe headaches, Marilyn went to a doctor who prescribed pain medication. One day she mistakenly took a second dose of the pills, forgetting she had already taken her daily allotment. Then, my daughter drove herself to work.

A short time later in the bakery section, Marilyn noticed that strange things were happening inside her head. Besides feeling extremely weak, her vision was becoming blurred as confusion and disorientation set in.

"I'm sick. I'm going to drive myself to the hospital," she told a fellow employee as she grabbed her purse and headed for her car.

She had gone a block or two when she saw a phone booth on the corner. Realizing her need for immediate help, Marilyn stopped her compact vehicle, hurried to the booth and dialed the number of an adjacent community's Drug Hotline.

"Something's wrong with me," she stammered to the person on the other end of the line. "What should I do?"

"Stay where you are!" came the reply. "An ambulance is on its way."

In the meantime, the store telephoned me about my daughter's condition. I hurried to the hospital's Emergency Room, but Marilyn wasn't there.

"We received a call from the Drug Hotline," the nurse began, "and they said an ambulance was bringing in someone named Marilyn who'd taken an overdose of medication."

I was so frightened for my daughter that my heart pounded. Please, God, see that someone is looking over my child, I prayed. Then, I waited.

But no one came. Not the ambulance and not Marilyn. Finally, I decided to go home in case my daughter was there. What if she's trying to call me? I worried.

After voicing my concern to the nurse on duty, I hurried out the door. My pulse raced as I negotiated the mid-morning traffic, and I prayed through my tears.

Once inside my house, I walked the floor and prayed outloud for my child. "Oh, Lord, Marilyn's in trouble and I don't know what to do. I'm placing her into your hands now, so it's all up to you. Please, take care of her!"

All at once, a feeling of peace enveloped me, closing about me like the arms of a sheer umbrella, wrapping itself around me. I became calm and every bit of fear left my body. I remember thinking, I don't know where my child is, but I know she's all right.

It was only moments before the phone rang. When I lifted the receiver a pleasant voice said, "I just called you, Mrs. Richardet, to let you know that your daughter is safe. She's at home."

My heart jumped for joy, and I rattled off a "thank you!" But I really wanted to add, "I already know!"

Then, without even a hint as to who the lady was or where she was calling from, the woman hung up. I wondered about that!

Later when I asked Marilyn what had happened that day, she said, "Actually, other than making the phone call to the Hotline, I don't remember anything until I found myself back in the safety of my own home. As sick and disorientated as I was, there's no way I could have driven the two miles home without help. I even parked the car in my usual spot on the driveway, but I don't recall doing that either."

In my heart I know that my prayers were answered. Because of God's great love for us, I believe that God or an angel became Marilyn's Helper Through The Haze that day.

Just who was the gentle-voiced woman who called, knowing that Marilyn was home? Could She have been someone who calls Heaven "home"?

Knowing that angels are mentioned no less than three hundred times in the Bible, we can be sure that these spirits interact with humans continuously, even today. It is only on certain occasions that they choose to be seen.

JESUS LOVES JESSICA!

by

Clairice Hetzler

Jessica was only two months old when Dave and I, along with our three grown sons, welcomed her into our home and our hearts. The innocent victim of probable abuse, the baby suffered from multiple head traumas that had already damaged her neurological system. Besides showing signs of severe mental retardation and cerebral palsy, the precious little girl quaked with tremors and startled infant jerks.

Not only was Jessica cordically blind, but she was unable to grasp objects with her tiny fingers. Her head was smaller than normal; still, we enrolled her in the "Birth To Three Years" program at our fine mental health facility. We prayed for her everyday and supported her in every way possible.

By the fall of 1992 when Jessica was eighteen months old, her seizures were identified as being of the multiple complex variety. Lying down was so uncomfortable for her that our family took turns holding her upright and close to our bodies. Sometimes, Jessica even stopped breathing as seizures came and went as they pleased, day and night. Medications prescribed by doctors sometimes helped for awhile, but never cured the little girl we had come to love and hoped to adopt. Because there were legal impediments at the time, that would have to wait.

There was cause for additional prayers when the doctors told us, "Jessica's body simply cannot survive these tremors forever." Still, I refused to give up on this child who had no self-help skills and counted on me to feed her up to six times a day.

At one of her doctor appointments, the physician told me, "Let's put a G tube in Jessica to feed her. It's taking too much of your time."

"I have the time!" I assured him, knowing that I had the support of a wonderful family, friends and fellow church members. Of course, the going wasn't always easy, but this child who needed us had strengthened not only our family bonds, but our faith, as well. Jessica was worth anything we had to do to make her life worth living.

Eventually, we moved to Charlotte, North Carolina, and we had to admit the little girl to a hospital for something other than neurological reasons. As it turned out, it was a blessing because her toxicity level was dangerously high, twice as high as it should have been, and medication was the culprit. Immediately, this three-year-old child, who was at the developmental stage of a normal three-month-old infant, was put on IVs.

After that crisis, Jessica began utilizing physical therapy again, as well as her special equipment at home. Then, by October 1993 when we were finally in the process of adoption, the little girl's seizures became continuous. Even touching her would throw her into one; so I would sit, quietly rocking and cuddling her, praying, thinking, crying.

Her medicine was changed. Finally, in December, it was official! Dave and I were the proud parents of Jessica, the child who even now was reverting back to the fetal position. As Dave stood holding her in his arms at her baptism, she suffered seizures. I imagine those in the congregation assumed that the tears that ran down my cheeks reflected sadness. No! They were tears of joy. Jessica was finally ours.

A month later, a miracle drug was prescribed for our new daughter and for the first time in her short life, Jessica was free of tremors, seizures and jerks. She still remained curled in the fetal position, with no control of her body, not even her head.

Since our family had discovered that praying for Jessica was as normal as breathing, we decided to turn to our church.

On March 23, 1994 at a Wednesday evening service, our pastor asked a group of those who were standing around us to lay hands on our daughter for God's healing. Together with the entire congregation of several hundred members, we prayed fervently.

But nothing changed, and we went home.

Two days later, I received a note from the teacher at the mental health facility. "Jessica smiled today!" she wrote. I was elated since the child hadn't done that in more than five months.

Over the next four months, Jessica improved rapidly. She became more responsive and tried to hold her head up. She ate better and gained nine pounds, all the while, smiling and happy with her surroundings. Her visible tremors and seizures had not reappeared. God was doing His part!

Jessica is still impaired, but we have learned never to look past where we are! I thank God everyday for our loving daughter who has good head control and a straight body. Her sight has improved, and she smiles all the time. Many of our friends now admit they had given up on Jessica's surviving the really scary times of three to four years ago. But I never gave up, and today my heart leaps with joy whenever I see my little girl scooting and rolling all over the floor. She laughs and babbles what she likes and dislikes as she tries to get around in her walker. The doctors cannot believe what they're seeing.

But if they knew the power of prayerful intercession, they would believe, as I do, that miracles occur everyday!

The terrible things that happened to our precious Jessica when she was a newborn are, of course, extremely sad. But sadness is no longer a part of our daughter's life. Happiness has taken it's place simply because Jesus loves Jessica! And so do we!

Chapter 6

Mary, Mercy and the Little Flower

Ever since Our Lady first appeared to Juan Diego at Guadalupe in 1531 and left her image behind on the poor Indian's cape, until the present day when she continues to appear at Medjugorje and other lesser known places around the world, Mary has identified herself as, "I am the Immaculate Virgin, the Queen of Heaven, the Immaculate Conception, the Mother of God, etc."

In 1933 at Beauraing, Belgium she instructed the seers to "Pray. Pray very much." Later, she uttered what was considered to be the Great Promise, "I will convert sinners."

The Lady did not say that she would ask God to convert them. No, "I will convert sinners," she said. What tremendous influence Mary must have with her Son. What tremendous power she must have as Queen of Heaven and Earth, the Mediatrix of All Graces—the channel through which all our prayers and requests are funneled to God, and the same channel through which God redirects all His graces to us. The dogma of Mary's Universal Mediation has not yet been confirmed by the Church, but most theologians accept the idea.

As do many of the Blessed Virgin Mary's followers who believe in their powerful, caring and loving Heavenly Mother. God will not refuse Her anything. So why not go through her for all of our favors?

AN ANGEL, A ROSE AND MERCY

by
Gloria Gebhardt

As I waited the beginning of morning Mass, my thoughts drifted to five years ago when the Lord led me to the St. Vincent's charismatic prayer group to foster my spiritual growth. There I take my role as part-time teacher seriously, but the week's lesson was slow coming together. The Bible verse kept eluding me and I had to remind myself to wait upon the Lord to supply the text.

Next, my thoughts settled softly on my favorite Uncle Milton, 64 years old and 14 years my senior. He was the brother I never had, but a day earlier I received the sad news that he was dying of a cancer that recurred after a remission. They said his time was short and that physically everything that could be done was being done. What about his spiritual needs?

Uncle Milly, his three brothers and three sisters were raised Catholic by German parents. But, somewhere between Missouri's corn fields and the Korean War, for unknown reasons, he had stopped going to church. This concerned his mother, Mary, and his return to the sacraments of the Catholic Church was a prayer she was praying on her January 1965 death bed.

Milly's sweetheart of a wife Doe, a devout Catholic, who had passed away recently from the same cancer, had petitioned a similar prayer. Friends of Doe's neighborhood church and family members urged Milly to return to the fold, but he had no use for the Church and their words fell on deaf ears.

Uncle Milly, the father of three, was a retired painter who lived a simple life. He enjoyed people, helped them and yet, something embittered him. He didn't need God and now, he was dying! I wondered how he would ever endure the suffering yet to come if he hadn't made peace with the Lord. How could he meet death? As difficult as it was for me to think about, I reminded myself that God was in control. Perhaps there was something he wanted me to do for my uncle.

Should I phone him? No! Long distance conversations seemed rushed and I needed time to bring up God's name. A personal visit? No, what if it made him uncomfortable? What if pushing religion upset him?

Lost in thought, I jumped when a hand touched my shoulder.

"This is for you," my friend whispered as she handed me an angel bookmark crocheted in shiny gold thread. "I've had it for several weeks, and I'm not sure where it came from. But I know of your fondness for angels and I wanted to pass it on to you."

Believing as I do that God sends signs and insights to let me know He is with me, I caressed the angel, ever thankful and aware that it was part of his plan that would unfold in God's time.

The next day I chose Luke 15:10 for my Bible Study group that night. "I tell you, there will be the same kind of joy before the angels of God over one repentant sinner." As I shared my reasons for selecting the angel reading with my group, I told them of Uncle Milly. All at once, I sensed the Holy Spirit allowing me the sight of something in my mind's eye. It was the word HERO.

Suddenly, my heart took flight with an idea, one that might make me look foolish for stating my beliefs, but one that could possibly open Milly's heart to God's love.

I could not brush paint into a new creation as He could, but after praying to the Holy Spirit for words and guidance at 3:00 p.m., the exact hour commemorating the Lord's death, His Hour of Divine Mercy, I picked up a willing pen and pushed it into the motion and form of a love letter.

Dear Uncle Milly,

Time slips away, often taking opportunities along with it, lost forever. I don't want to miss my opportunity, feeble though it is, to bring about good. So, from across many summertime miles, I travel with pen in hand to be with you to speak of matters of the heart.

Experts say the world is in turmoil because children no longer have heroes they can look up to. I was luckier than kids of today. I believe the reason the Lord allowed you to survive your fall into the barnyard cistern as a toddler was so you could grow up to become my hero. To me, the mark of a hero is giving of self. From earliest memories you did just that. Whether putting worms on my hook for serious cane pole fishing, allowing me to help Turtle Wax your prized black Chevy or sitting at Grandma's dinner table chomping crispy, Sunday-fried chicken, being with you lent specialness to ordinary events. You had a way of making me feel important. If I was a pest, you never let on. A hero wouldn't.

Do you remember the white chenille housecoat with the colorful peacock you brought me from Korea? It was the gift of gifts! I wore it until it no longer fit; then I hung it on a hook on my closet door as a reminder of you. It aged with me.

Winds of time blew my direction moving me through adolescence and into adulthood. Times spent with you were fewer but each remained a special time.

On my wedding day, to please me, you swallowed your distaste for church to usher guests down the long aisle. You gave of self, a deed a hero would do.

You introduced my husband and children to your great love, the outdoors. You welcomed us to your cabin in the Ozark hills where tales of nature warmed our hearts and tickled our funny bones with good times.

You came to our aid when we purchased our first house by offering to spruce it up with new paint. Freely giving of time and self, you painted the whole thing!

Seasons of life continue to change but one thing will never change: the hero who lit up the green eyes of a curly, brown-haired little girl still warms the heart of the graying woman of today.

Uncle Milly, I need to ask you to perform one more heroic deed. Release whatever it is that has kept you from the Church all these years. Make peace with the Lord and receive the sacraments. I assume even heroes need to be strengthened at times. I read recently that Holy Communion is like Angel's Bread, food for the journey. I want you well nourished. Doing this would mean more to me than the cherished memory I have of the best gift I ever received, my peacock housecoat.

Someday I hope to be like you, someone's hero. Thank you for helping me become the person I am today.

Love,
Gloria Jean

I sealed the letter, sent it off on wings of angels and hoped it would soften my uncle's hardened heart. A week passed, two weeks! As Milly's condition deteriorated, I increased my prayers for him, reminding myself that God was in control.

On a hot humid Saturday morning in August when I was kneeling in the church in prayer for my uncle, a friend who was unaware of Milly's condition, scooted into the pew beside me. She handed me a red rose.

"This morning when I picked the rose, your name came to mind. I think the Lord wants you to have it," she whispered.

For an instant, I was dumbfounded. Then, tears filled my eyes, and I knew that the Holy Spirit was not only reassuring me that God was with me, but that God was caring for my uncle. The tiny rosebud smelled heavenly and reminded me of Saint Therese, the Little Flower. Was I to invoke the aid of this great saint on my uncle's behalf?

That day I began praying the Little Flower's Rosary Chaplet as well as the nine-day Novena of St. Therese, requesting a reconciliation of my uncle with the Lord and a peaceful, holy death. I prayed the Lord's mercy would wash Uncle Milly clean of sin, remembering that it is commonly believed that St. Therese often grants the sign of roses to those who practice her devotion as proof that their petition is granted.

"St. Therese, please send me a sign that Milly rests in the arms of Jesus," I begged.

Four days passed. Then, three more. On Sunday, the ninth and final day of my novena, my hero died at exactly three o'clock in the afternoon, the Hour of Our Lord's Divine Mercy. Tears filled my eyes! Not only had the Little Flower delivered a rose, she sent the "sign" and a whole garden of roses.

The following Wednesday in St. Rita's Church at Uncle Milly's funeral Mass my eyes were drawn, almost magnetically, to the radiant face of the Sacred Heart of Jesus. I was enveloped in peace as I sensed God reaffirming me that my uncle's soul now resided in the heart of the Lord. Later, as we were leaving the cemetery, my cousin Kim (Milly's daughter) hurried over to me and said, "I want to thank you, Jean, for the beautiful letter you wrote to Dad. He read it often and it helped him a lot. When I asked him what he wanted me to do with it, he told me 'Put it in my special box. I'll save it!'"

The Lord took care of everything, just like I knew He would. Praise His name!

1. "Faith is telling a mountain to move and being shocked only if it doesn't!"

FOUR YELLOW ROSES

by
Carlene Soebbing

The yellow roses in my garden were in full bloom that summer of 1985, or was it '84? Funny how the memories go. Anyway, it was the year that our youngest son Jerry came home from the Air Force on leave, and we had planned the biggest picnic yet. Everyone was invited, the entire clan, along with my good friend Bernadine, who lived at the Senior Citizens Complex.

For the occasion, I cleaned, cooked and, finally, plucked four of my finest blooms from the rose garden as a centerpiece. I was looking forward to having Bernadine as a guest. Since she was an only child and lived alone, I enjoyed having her over, along with her quick wit and infectious smile.

But on the morning of the big day, she phoned to apologize for not being able to attend the celebration. Her rheumatism was acting up. I was sorry, too, but Jerry was pulling up out front and everyone was waiting for dinner.

Afterwards, when my youngest daughter Mary and I were in the kitchen, I decided to fill a plate with leftovers for my ailing friend.

"Why not take her the four yellow roses, Mom? There's plenty more in the garden," Mary suggested.

The idea sounded wonderful. Quickly, I wrapped the golden roses inside a sheet of foil and, with both packages in hand, I headed for Indian Hills.

When Bernadine answered her door, she smiled. After she took the plate of food to the kitchen, she hurried back to where I sat on the couch, holding the flowers. Slowly, Bernadine peeled back the foil and began to cry, "I can't believe it! I can't believe it!"

"Is something wrong?" I stammered, confused because I knew how much my friend loved roses.

The older lady looked at me and reached deep into her pocket for a tissue. "The flowers are beautiful! No, nothing's wrong. It's just that . . . "

"Why are you crying?" I asked, afraid I had done something to hurt her feelings.

The teary-eyed woman cleared her throat. "When I asked Saint Therese, the Little Flower, for a special request, I also asked her to give me a sign."

"Yes?" By now, I was straining forward in my chair.

"A faint smile etched the woman's thin lips. "I asked the Little Flower to send either the aroma of roses or.," she hesitated, "Or to send someone bearing four yellow roses."

In the momentary silence and at a complete loss for words, we sat basking in God's presence in the room. It was so prominent that I could have reached out and touched the Lord, or Saint Therese. Inside, I thought, Thank you, dear God, for allowing me to be your instrument and messenger. I knew that, no matter what, God is always with us, whether we think so or not.

MARY AT MY WINDOW WATCHING

by

Ella Marie Reiter

As a convert to the Catholic faith, I often looked to my husband and others for support. Little did I know that my conversion would introduce me to a beautiful and powerful lady who goes by the name of the Blessed Virgin Mary. Once I began praying to her, she became my pillar of strength, and I quickly discovered that going through her was the surest and quickest way to her Son.

Let me tell you what our Heavenly Queen has done for me as I boast only of Her power and that of her Son, Jesus Christ.

In 1987, six years after they began, I read about the apparitions taking place in Medjugorje, Yugoslavia. The messages delivered by Mary so touched my heart that, on Ash Wednesday, I began praying the rosary daily for the conversion of souls. Also I began the practice of making the five first Saturdays, along with saying its five decades of the rosary, going to confession and meditating fifteen minutes on all fifteen mysteries of the rosary. The five First Saturdays, a practice I've continued to this day, was a request of Our Lady at Fatima. Through them, she promises help at the hour of death with all of the graces needed for salvation. We honor and make reparation to the Immaculate Heart of Mary for all the blasphemies and ingratitudes of men.

The Blessed Mother has heard my vow to continue this practice until my death to make up for all the years that I ignored her, especially the first twenty-five years of my Catholic life.

January 1988—Here I added the practice of saying the Fifteen Prayers of St. Bridget. When said daily for 365 days, these fifteen prayers honor the 5480 blows given to Christ's body during the overall time of the Crucifixion. There are wonderful privileges promised to all who say these prayers devoutly everyday for one year. I look forward to saying them daily.

In 1989 the Invocation in Honor of the Holy Wounds of Our Lord Jesus Christ, the seven Our Fathers and seven Hail Marys in honor of the Sorrows of Mary and the Prayer To Saint Joseph became part of my prayer life. Then, in 1990, I began to say the fifteen-decade rosary daily, and I felt God's blessings (that came through Mary's intercession) pour into my life. I also found solace and privacy as I prayed in my bedroom.

That same year I discovered the Divine Mercy Devotions of Blessed Faustina Kowalska, wherein I recite the Chaplet of Mercy daily, especially for the dying, on my rosary beads, and remember the Three O'Clock Hour with prayers and meditation for the Hour of Great Mercy that reflects the horrors of Christ's Crucifixion. I also started making the Novena of Divine Mercy that begins on Good Friday and ends on Mercy Sunday, the first Sunday after Easter.

At about the same time, I decided to make the nine First Fridays, along with the First Saturdays, and this has been observed to this day.

The following years, 1991-92, saw me begin the Consecration to the Immaculate Heart of Mary Prayer and the Devotion to Honor the Sacred Heart of Jesus. (June is Sacred Heart month) I could feel my devotion growing daily to both the Sacred Heart of Jesus and the Immaculate Heart of Mary.

By 1993 I began to say the Chaplet of St. Michael to the nine choirs of angels, and before attending the Medjugorjean Conference, I started making, continuously on the special feast days, the 33-day Preparation for Total Consecration to Jesus through Mary according to St. Louis-Marie de

Montfort. That same year, I added The Two Divine Promises, a 30-day Communion Novena, which is done for the salvation of my soul and the souls of others. Each month this novena allows me to include my intentions for one or two other people. (When you break a novena, you should begin it again until you finish the required number of days.) I have been able to make these novenas each month for three years without breaking them. Thank you, dear Lord!

At this point, my prayer life was blossoming, thanks to Mary and Jesus. Then, something unexpected happened!

On September 2, 1993 I went to confession at St. Boniface Church. When I entered Father John Carberry's confessional box and knelt down, the panel slid open and the priest's voice sounded unusually loud and authoritative as he was giving me his greeting. Since the tone of voice I heard was quite unlike what I would expect from Father Carberry, I assumed that another priest had taken his place. After confessing my faults, the priest started to give me absolution, but it seemed as if the strong voice I'd heard before had made a transition back to the more familiar and quiet voice of Father Carberry, that was often hard to hear.

As I knelt in the dimness, I was shocked to hear Father Carberry's voice behind the screen. I tried to rationalize why he sounded so different. Perhaps he had a cold? No! As I listened, I realized it was Father's normal voice.

Moments later as I pondered this powerful experience, I remembered reading in Blessed Faustina's Divine Mercy In My Soul Diary that Jesus had told her "In the Sacreament of Reconciliation (Confession), I am only hidden by the priest. I myself act in your soul. He is, for Me, only a screen." Knowing that Blessed Faustina had experienced hearing Our Lord's voice through her confessor, and having all the knowledge of how this can happen, I knew that Jesus, through the personage of Father Carberry, had miraculously spoken to me that day. Praise be to God!

Ten days later when I met with Father Carberry, I told him what I had experienced. I asked him if he had noticed anything different that day in the confessional and he admitted that his voice had become louder at one point during confessions, thereby, confirming my belief that the Lord had spoken to me through my confessor.

It was then that Father asked me if I wanted him to be my spiritual advisor. That's when Father John Carberry, pastor of St. Boniface Church, came into my life, and I've been grateful ever since.

During these years I grew spiritually, and many blessings found their way into our home as the children grew up and began to leave the nest. My husband John and I actually looked forward to being a couple again. Around this time, through the intercession of the Blessed Mother, Father Carberry asked me if I would like to attend a Legion of Mary meeting. On February

8, 1994 when I became an active member of the group, John was there to share my joy.

Another amazing chapter of my life opened on February 20, 1994. As I awaited the arrival of my replacement at the Perpetual Adoration Chapel, the memory of hearing the Lord's voice in the confessional still fresh in my mind, a young man stopped in for a visit. As we spoke, he seemed to be so holy that I wondered, Dear Jesus, is this you in disguise?

Ironically, it was through this conversation that I was led to St. Boniface Church to meet the young man's mother, Ruth Holman. She confirmed the identity of this devout person as being her son Mark, and explained that another son had offered to pay for her and a guest to go to Lourdes. To my surprise, she invited me, a stranger, to accompany her on the pilgrimage. I was ecstatic. It had been less than 24 hours since my conversation with Mark first took place. Ruth and I immediately saw the Blessed Mother's hand in making this all possible.

But before the September trip, Ruth had to undergo emergency surgery. I felt very close to the family, and when her son phoned and asked me to pray for his mother, I remembered my new friend to the Blessed Virgin Mary with prayers and devotions that were answered with a successful surgery. The trip was on!

Carefully, I filled a backpack with religious articles and prayer cards from friends and family alike, intending to carry this as a penance for their personal burdens. Because of the miraculous way I was asked on the trip, I knew that extra graces would come to all. As I walked the holy land of Portugal and France, I planned to ask God's blessings on those back home.

On a cool September 24th Ruth and I left on the pilgrimage. After stopping in Lisbon, Portugal we visited the birthplace of St. Anthony of Padua, the Lisbon Cathedral, the Monastery of St. Jeronimo and Belem Tower. In Santarem we attended Mass at the Church of the Holy Miracle where the venerated Relic of the "Bleeding Host" has been kept since 1269. I had the privilege of venerating and kissing the Pyx, the glass container which encloses the host. Praise be to God for this holy moment.

At Fatima we participated in the rosary and candlelight procession from the Chapel of Apparitions on the Cove Da Iria where the Blessed Virgin appeared to the three children, Francisco, Jacinta and Lucia, for the first time on May 13, 1917, (passing the Basilica enroute.) The procession returned to the Chapel where the candles I carried in the names of my friends were placed into special holders where they would stay.

We saw St. Anthony's Parish Church in which the three children were baptized, the original graves of Francisco and Jacinta (who died at a young age) but who now rest in the Basilica, as well as the homes of the two deceased visionaries. I laid articles and petitions on Francisco's death bed.

Next we traveled to the former home of Lucia, who is now a cloistered nun residing in Coimbra, where her bedroom was blocked off by glass. Down the path at the Holy Well where the Angel of Peace appeared to the children, I placed the backpack of items for special blessings. Then, after stopping at the cave where the Angel gave the seers Communion and where the messenger urged them to pray and make sacrifices for sinners, we walked to the statue where the Blessed Virgin Mary appeared to the children (after their release from prison) and told them to recite the rosary daily. In order to prove the authenticity of her apparitions and to make the world believe, Our Lady performed a miracle. On October 13, 1917 over seventy thousand people looked up in wonder and witnessed what has come to be known as "The Miracle Of The Sun."

When we visited Lucia's Carmelite Convent the following day in Coimbra, we attended Mass in the chapel. During the liturgy, I experienced feelings that are difficult to explain, knowing that the Virgin Mary had appeared to Lucia, who was somewhere in the building at that moment. Before Mass a basket had been passed for our petitions, petitions for which Sister Lucia herself would pray. Oh, what blessings will come from these prayers, I thought.

After leaving the convent, we visited the University of Coimbra and St. Clair's Monastery where the casket containing the incorrupt body of the beloved St. Elizabeth lies just above and behind the chapel's altar. A statue of the saint overlooks the city.

On our way back to Fatima, Ruth glanced out the window of the bus, pointed and cried, "Look!"

All heads turned in her direction. "I see it!" another woman shouted. Then I stammered, "So do I!" my nose pressed against the glass.

Above us, the midday sun began to spin, pulsating with bright, flashing lights. At first, it descended toward us. Then, it retreated and began to change from green to pink to blue, all with a golden-yellow hue that spread outward from the center. Finally, the sun returned to normal.

We looked around, but soon discovered that not everyone had witnessed the phenomenon, not even the priest seated behind me. For some reason, only a few of us had sampled a view of the Miracle of the Sun that happened in 1917.

We continued on to Burgos, Spain where we attended Mass. Then, our bus stopped at Lourdes, France, one of the world's greatest pilgrimage shrines where five million visitors go annually. On February 11, 1858 the Blessed Virgin Mary appeared to Bernadette Soubirous near a grotto. She instructed the young girl to dig a hole from which sprang water that has flowed ever since and has, on occasions, been the source of miracles. There are baths and fountains for visitors, and thousands immerse themselves in the holy water. For additional blessings, I held the religious articles under the fountain, and left the petitions in a container in the Grotto. (Later I discovered some petitions had been answered even before I returned home.) I also brought back several quarts of holy water with me.

That evening we participated in a candlelight procession and the rosary. The next morning we attended Mass at St. Gabriel's Chapel, located near the Basilica and Rosary Cathedral. Not far away is the world's largest underground church, the Basilica of St. Pius X that seats 27,000, and after a brief visit there, we toured the homes in which Bernadette lived, including the prison where she was forced to stay during the time of the apparitions. Then, we boarded a sleeper train for Paris.

There we visited the Shrine of the Miraculous Medal where, on November 27, 1830, the Blessed Virgin appeared to St. Catherine Labouré to give her the design and instructions on how to have a medal produced in her honor. Over the years, many blessings, graces and miracles have been received from the wearing of this medal. Saint Catherine's incorrupt body lies in a casket at the front of the chapel next to the chair on which the Blessed Mother sat when she appeared to her.

Then, it was time to return to America. At Kennedy airport in New York, when we changed planes for our trip to St. Louis, there were so many vacancies on the flight that we had our choice of seats. I chose one on the aisle. It was three o'clock in the afternoon, the Hour of Great Mercy, and I was immersed in my prayers.

A man stopped beside me. "I think you're in my seat," he said quietly. Startled, I reached beneath the cushion for my backpack, but all I felt was air. My precious carrier and items were missing and our flight was about to leave.

As I explained my problem to the flight attendants, I realized that I must have left the pack on the shuttle we had taken from the other plane. I rushed back to the terminal where a desk attendant phoned the shuttle driver. The backpack was sitting there, untouched. Praise God, was all I could think as I ran the quarter mile, each way, in order to retrieve my backpack and get back to my seat, with a few minutes to spare. Several hours later, our plane landed safely on the ground in St. Louis, but my heart seemed to remain airborne for a very long time.

As the days passed and I returned to my routine life, I kept ignoring several thin rusty lines of colored moisture that were making stains on the outer edges of our bedroom's Priscilla tie-backs. I assumed that when I watered the hanging plant that dangled along side of the window, the pot overflowed enough to drip moisture onto the ruffled ivory curtains. Even one of the tie-backs had an unusual looking blotch on it.

It's time to put them in the laundry, I told myself, but for some unknown reason, I procrastinated.

Then, on November 9, 1994, only a month after my pilgrimage to Lourdes/Fatima, I was praying one day while seated on the edge of our bed. Suddenly, I noticed something unusual staring back at me from the raised fold of our discolored window covering.

I gaped at the image that confronted me, trying to discern what I was actually seeing. Obviously, it was some kind of figure.

Being familiar with pictures of Our Lady of Guadalupe, the resemblance seemed strikingly similar. The dark and light areas, the contours, the perfect mantle and the aurora around her. (Father John Carberry says, "Since the image of Our Lady of Guadalupe has never changed for over 400 years, and is approved by the Church, it is considered a supernatural phenomenon.")

The power of the effigy left me stunned. I sat there trying to comprehend what had just transpired in my bedroom.

A week later, after watering the plant, I studied the image on the curtain. Another stain, in a rounded form and shape, had run down to the tip of the aurora. The more defined lines of the figure's base had changed.

It was then that I looked up to see fresh sap on the end of one of the plant's broken stems—Our Lady was using this simple shaft as her brush and the sap as the paint.

I began to share the Blessed Mother's handiwork with all who wished to bask in its presence. (Father Carberry comments, "In some ways, the stain resembles Our Lady of Fatima or, possibly, Our Lady of Guadalupe, or it could be a combination of several since the Virgin appears in many ways.")

In July 1995 Sister Elizabeth Mast S.F.P. visited our bedroom, and in her letter she says, "I visited Ella Marie Reiter's home to see the figure left on the curtain by a dripping flower hanging near the window. Since I'm a person who would normally question an alleged figure like this, I was happy to see it. Mary Courty and I visited Ella together, and having visited the shrine of Our Lady of Guadalupe in Mexico, I could immediately detect the dark and lighter areas of sunlight around the form that could resemble Our Lady of Guadalupe. The area above the image could certainly represent the cloud in the sky with its rounded form and shape."

And Father Carberry adds, "Because of the dripping from the plant, I believe this is only a natural phenomenon."

Eventually, I was forced to remove the "weeping" plant from our bedroom. No! I haven't done the laundry yet, nor will I ever wash the image left on the curtain by Our Blessed Mother. I enjoy her presence everyday as I pray with Mary At My Window Watching. (Her picture is on the cover)

ABOUT THE HOUR OF MERCY (AND MORE)

Devotion to either our Lord of Mercy or Mary, Mother of Mercy, involves a total commitment to them as Mercy. It is our decision to trust them completely, accept their mercy with thanksgiving, and be merciful as They are merciful.

At the Three O'Clock Hour each day, the time recalling Christ's death on the Cross, there are many who stop to pray, if only for a moment. In His revelations to Blessed Faustina Kowalska, Our Lord asked for special prayers and veneration for his Passion and to implore His mercy, especially for sinners, during this time.

For additional information on the Hour of Mercy, please call: 1-800-462-7426.

St. Louis-Marie de Montfort says, "Giving our life totally to Mary and to Jesus through Mary, is a short road to finding Jesus Christ."

"We make more progress in a brief period of submission to and dependence on Mary, than in whole years of following our own will and relying upon ourselves."

"It is true that we can attain divine union by other roads, but it is by many crosses and strange deaths, and with many more difficulties which we shall find it hard to overcome."

Our Lady has promised great graces to all who wear her Miraculous Medal around their necks. Originally known as the Medal of the Immaculate Conception, the name was changed to reflect the wonders it has worked. St. Catherine Labouré was the only seer ever to be allowed to kneel with her hands resting on Mary's lap as they chatted for long periods of time.

~ CHAPTER 7 ~

This Is God Speaking!
(Dreams: In and Out-Of-Body)

> "For God does speak, perhaps once, or even twice, though one perceive it not. In a dream, in a vision of the night, [when deep sleep falls upon men] as they slumber in their beds, It is then he opens the ears of men . . . '
>
> (Job 33:14-16)

Forty-seven years ago and long before people spoke readily about out-of-body experiences, Edna Runser remembers having one. Unfortunately, many details have been lost over the years, but she vividly recalls that night when she and her best girlfriend were headed on foot for their high school's basketball game.

It was a cold winter's night and the softly falling snow quickly covered the icy sidewalks. It wasn't long before Edna's feet slipped. She fell and landed on her back and head. After getting up, she assumed no damage had been done, so the friends continued on to the big game. Later, they returned home.

The next several hours have been wiped from Edna's memory but when she woke up in the Emergency Room of a Hannibal hospital, she suddenly felt herself floating upward off the gurney on which she had been lying. Her weightless self continued to rise into the air until she found herself in a corner of the room that was brilliantly light.

"I was dressed in white," Edna remembers. "And down below me, in what I would describe as normal illumination, I could see a group of people working on someone. It was me!"

At that point, Edna's memory fades. Over the years, she seldom discussed the incident, but she does remember that when she awoke, she discovered that she had been seriously ill with pneumonia in the hospital for several days.

THE DAY I MET MY GUARDIAN ANGEL (A Heartbeat from Paradise)

by
Billie Brod

The day our youngest son was born was the day, I believe, that I first encountered my guardian angel's presence. At the time, I anticipated having natural childbirth, but God had other plans.

I was in the delivery room. Contractions were intense as I bore down, wishing our newborn would hurry. Still, I sensed something was wrong when I heard the doctor and nurses saying things like, "the baby shifted into an impossible position," and "he's trying to be born chest-first; his head and chin are pushed backwards."

The pain was unbearable when, suddenly, I went into convulsions and passed out.

Seconds later, I was outside my body, floating somewhere above myself in an illuminated corner of the delivery room. A bright figure stood beside me, and even though I didn't turn around, I felt his arm wrapped about my shoulders. From his touch came indescribable peace and joy. It was as if we were communicating inaudibly.

Everything will be all right. Don't worry, I felt him telling me. Together, we watched as the doctor pushed my son back enough to get the head into proper birth position. As the baby came into the world, I noticed a concave depression in the front of his forehead.

"If this baby makes it, he could very well suffer brain damage," the gynecologist commented.

I should have been frightened at the prospect, but the spirit at my side kept assuring me that my child would be fine. "Don't worry!" I kept hearing inside myself.

At that point, the angel tugged at my shoulder, attempting to turn me away from the scene, as if leading me somewhere else, hopefully, toward Heaven.

"No! I can't leave Bob with three small children!" I tried to say. At that instant, when I was but a heartbeat from Paradise, I found myself back on the table, inside my body. The anesthesiologist was saying, "She's back!"

Around me, the pace was frantic. Our family doctor worked on our baby, while both the anesthesiologist and doctor worked on me. Praise God, both mother and son survived the ordeal.

And thank you, God, and my Guardian Angel for ministering to me in that brilliantly-lit area of the delivery room and all you have done for both of us. Our beautiful red-headed son was not only undamaged, but graduated top of his class at his school of aeronautics.

WITH EVERY BEAT OF MY HEART

by
Jan Faler

In 1966 I first underwent open-heart surgery, so in looking back over the years, I remember thoughts like:

Oh, no! Here we go again! I wonder if my heart will shape up on its own or does this mean another trip to the hospital? Who can we call to watch our little girls? I don't want them to be scared. Maybe if I just ignore it, this time it won't be so bad. What if I stayed still? Would walking around help? Boy, I don't want to have to call Lawson at work!

There were thoughts about pills—did I take all my medication? Another Quinidex? Gosh, my stomach is already icky from all that medicine.

Then, I'd talk to God—"Dear Lord, it's so difficult to pray when I need you the most. Please take care of my heart and put it back into rhythm. Please, be with all of us and keep us safe."

So many times, since I've become a mother, the scene these comments conjure up, and others very similar, depict my life as it was for many years. My damaged heart often flips out of rhythm to interrupt both my day's activities as well as my night's sleep. The endings to the scenes have varied. Sometimes my heart converts back to sinus rhythm and I can continue with what I'm doing. Other times, I might take one or two of the medications and wait, perhaps minutes or hours or, sometimes, even days for my heart to shape up again.

As you can imagine, a chronic heart condition often sent us scurrying to the doctor. Sometimes the physician came to our house, even in the middle of the night. When my medicines failed to do their job, an I.V. usually took care of the problem. My face was familiar to most Emergency Room personnel who often admitted me to the hospital for additional treatment.

The part that bothered me most was how upsetting my illness was to our two little girls, Laura and Kendall. They were aware that Daddy often had to take care of everybody, and they grew accustomed to being suddenly dropped off at either Aunt Mary's or Grandma Nellie's whenever my condition warranted it. It don't know what we would have done without all our families' help!

No matter how positive I tried to be in front of our little ones, fear could never be hidden from those closest to me. Sometimes, I was very afraid! Other times, I was more sad than scared, and it was easy to sense similar emotions in my husband and daughters. The years passed and my heart continued to misbehave. I worried that I'd not live long enough to see my two children grow up.

"I want to raise my daughters!" I told God, my family and a few close friends. I tried to do things I thought a mother should have the privilege to do for those she loved. But I often became short of breath easily and my doctor's usual advice upon leaving his office was, "Lounge around a bit!"

I tried to follow his orders but it was frustrating, especially when no one knew exactly what could trigger an attack. They happened just as often when I was doing nothing (or sleeping) as they did when I was busy. Of course, I avoided physical activities like sports, running, etc., although I always danced a bit at wedding receptions, even on the night our first child Laura was born.

Once when Laura was four, I remember having to run across the street with her hand in mine to keep from getting hit in traffic. On the far curb, she laughed and giggled, "Mommy, I didn't know you could run!"

I wanted to cry. Instead, I giggled along with her so we could enjoy that precious moment. After all, I didn't know how long I would be around to enjoy such innocence and light.

Then, too, my husband was a very athletic young man who had lots of energy. It would have been nice to share golf, hiking, and baseball games with him and the kids. But we adjusted and considered it a small price to pay if only I could live to raise my two beautiful little girls. O, please, Lord!

Then one night when the girls were grade-school age, I awoke from a very sound sleep. Suddenly, an image appeared on what I'd describe as the crystal lenses of my eyes. It was a painting, a portrait, as it were, of two beautiful young women in profile, one a brunette and the other a blond. Instantly I recognized the women in the vision as our little brunette Laura and our little blond Kendall, all grown up.

At that moment, I felt calmness and joy overwhelming me. God's sign, this vision, was His promise that, one day, I'd see my two youngsters as grown-up women. Yes, I'd be there! And in that unexpected moment of realization, I smiled outloud, if that's possible.

And the Lord has kept his promise! Laura and Kendall have both graduated from school, married wonderful husbands and blossomed into the beautiful women I saw years ago in the vision. Not only have I been blessed to share their lives, I'm also Grandma Jan to several wonderful grandchildren.

No, my heart hasn't changed its ways. It still flip-flops around at will—sometimes, a lot, sometimes, not so much. I have had a second open-heart surgery, regular checkups, many pills and prayers to keep me going, and I try to view life as a piece of cake.

The frosting on that beautiful cake is that I'm now able to be very active. Our grandchildren know me as a person who can pitch and catch balls, play in swimming pools on long, hot afternoons, walk pretty fast and far, even in cold weather, in order to Christmas Carol from door to door, and I even keep up with an energetic husband who plays golf, although I swing a few more times than he does.

We have been blessed to sing together as husband and wife, as a family, and in choirs and choruses. Most of our music is Christian because we want the world to know Jesus as we know Him.

With every breath of my lungs, I want to acknowledge Him! With Every Beat Of My Heart, I want to love Him!

I depend on Him! I lean on Him! I praise, thank and glorify him!

For a long time, Jan was unable to share her vision with anyone, not even her husband Lawson. She cherished the secret as a special gift given to her by God to see them through the stormy times her body would put her through. The calmness she received that night helped greatly in quieting her heart during erratic episodes. Even though God has not yet healed Jan's damaged but loving heart, He has always held it protectively in the palm of his hand!

HEART TO HEART

by

Carmela Simone

(Not Real Name)

I was born and raised a Catholic in Cleveland, Ohio where we lived in a modest bungalow, just two doors away from our parish church. I remember the Masses and the novenas, as well as my wonderful Italian family who used their hands a lot while speaking, and who hugged a lot whenever they felt like it. Yes, the Simones had a real and great zest for life. Unfortunately, when I was only thirteen, I almost threw mine away.

For whatever reasons, real or imaginary, I had become a truly unhappy person. In fact, my sadness had moved past the port of unhappiness and I was sinking in a sea of depression.

One day I foolishly tried to escape my plight and pain by downing a half bottle of aspirins. I waited—one hour, two hours. It was still late afternoon, and nothing was happening. By eight o'clock that evening, I wondered what had taken place when I wasn't even feeling queasy in my stomach.

I couldn't tell anyone what I had tried to do, but still, I was confused as to why I was still alive. That night I went to bed at the regular time and quickly fell asleep.

During the night it seemed as if something was summoning me out of a deep slumber. I sensed a rush of reality, and yet I was in bed. This has to be connected with a dream, I told myself. Yet, everything seemed so vivid, so clear.

Suddenly, I was standing at our kitchen window, looking out through the venetian blinds. I gasped at the sight of seeing someone, dressed and hazy in white, standing on the roof of our garage. Quickly, I opened the door and scurried out onto the back porch.

Slowly, the figure on the garage floated down toward where I stood on the painted boards. When He was no more than six feet in front of me, the beautiful apparition stopped. Instantly, I knew who it was.

It was Jesus and He had come to see me. I had to catch my breath when I noticed His Sacred Heart, crowned with thorns and bleeding, burning with the flames of love and beating against the garments on his chest.

I must be awake, I told myself, as I stared at the face and form of my Savior. I was speechless, but He wasn't!

Standing before me with His arms wide open and outward, Jesus said in a clear, soft voice, "Child, what have you done? Do you know it's not time for you?"

Then, He folded his hands as if praying and moved them up and down as He continued, "I have many things you need to do yet. I have plans for you!"

With that, the Sacred Heart of Jesus floated backward and vanished from sight.

I was still in bed, but I was drawing myself into a sitting, and then a running position as I hurried through the dark house toward the kitchen window. Hopefully, I glanced out through the blinds.

But there was nothing to see. Jesus was gone.

As I drew a glass of water to drink, I sighed and, slowly, made my way back to my bed.

The minute my head rested on the pillow, I sensed a comforting peace and a new confidence coming over me. It allowed me to view myself and the world in a whole new light, the light of the Almighty.

Softly, I prayed and thanked the Sacred Heart of Jesus for the unexpected Heart to Heart. Ever since that night, my prayer life has increased and the Lord has protected me and showered my family and me with so many wonderful blessings.

Praise you, Jesus! Praise you!

After reading this story, one can reasonably assume that Jesus had already begun His encounter with the adolescent when He, not only saved her life, but chose to save her from having any adverse minor side effects from the enormous overdose of pills.

REMEMBER—THE ONLY WAY TO STAY CLEAR OF SATAN IS TO STAY CLOSE TO GOD!

THE LADY IN PINK

by

Genevia "Sue" Osborne

In the summer of 1995 I was shocked when we received word that my nephew Georgie had been seriously injured in a motorcycle accident. Since our families had always been very close, my immediate response was to fly to their sides, to help them and to allow them to draw on my strength. I wanted to comfort them all, especially Georgie and my brother who, surely, was aching as he sat at the bedside of his critically-ill son.

But I soon discovered that flying was out of the question. There were no flights to Springfield, Ohio and the only private plane was already booked. My remaining choice was to make the 8-hour trip by car and pray that I reached the hospital in time.

After packing my suitcase, I stopped by the living room where my husband was already seated on the couch. I joined him there for a brief respite, placed my head back against the heavy cushions and slowly closed my eyes.

It was then, with my eyes still shut, that I saw something with the reality of my mind's eye. A beautiful, featureless woman was floating up near the ceiling of our living room, and without speaking, the figure flew toward me, glowing brightly with the delicate softness of pink billowing clouds. I immediately recognized the vision—so familiar, so sweet. It was my mother who had died eight years earlier and who loved pink! She spoke to me in silence and I understood her to say, "I have come for Georgie. In fact, I am already with him, caring for him. Do not fear, Sue, your nephew is all right. I will lead him to the other side."

Instantly, I opened my eyes. My mother was gone but the reality of Georgie's impending death hit me and I stammered, "No! No! Don't take him!" Beads of perspiration dotted my forehead.

My husband suspected something special had just happened. As best I could, I described the experience of my mother's visit.

"You know how much Mom loved pink," I said. "I believe that she's with Georgie right now, preparing him and caring for him. Who better could the Lord have sent than a boy's grandmother!"

I grabbed my suitcase and drove to Ohio. At the Springfield city limits, I telephoned the hospital. When my niece answered the phone, she told me that Georgie had just passed away. Even though my heart was saddened, I had the consolation of knowing it was my angel mother who had led my nephew into Heaven's light.

When I reached the hospital room, I joined the other family members who sat quietly with Georgie. We shared our grief, prayed and said our goodbyes to a young man who was at peace, rejoicing with The Lady In Pink.

Later, as I left the hospital with my brother and his wife, I told them about the apparition and, with a forced, small smile on my lips, I gave them a big hug.

Despite the tremendous grief that weighed on their hearts in the loss of a son, the couple seemed to find some comfort in knowing that Georgie's grandmother was taking Georgie home with her that day.

And I thanked God for The Lady In Pink!

Genevia's love for angels of every kind is visible in her everyday life. Shortly after Georgie's death, she opened an angel shop and named it Genevia's Angel Haven. In it, she displayed angel figurines, dolls, ornaments, jewelry and other items with an angelic motif. One of Genevia's prized possessions, and one that is not for sale, is an angel figure dressed in pink.

~ Chapter 8 ~

The Great Physician

Evidence continues to grow showing that faith and religious belief can be good medicine and that it has positive effects on health. Doctors and medical students are gradually viewing the faith factor as an important health variable; they are beginning to see that if it is understood and utilized properly, it can have profound benefits for those who suffer.

Although this may be new to the medical profession, people of faith have long known about the healing power of the Great Physician. Jesus Christ healed thousands of afflicted bodies and minds while he ministered on earth, even to the point of bringing people back to life. Why shouldn't he continue this practice from Heaven? Didn't He allow Mary, his Mother, to provide us with the miraculous water of Lourdes?

> "Indeed, the whole crowd was trying to touch him because power went out from him which cured all."
>
> (Luke 6:19)

> And in (James 5:14–15) we read: "Is there anyone sick among you? He should ask for the presbyters of the church. They in turn are to pray over him, anointing him with oil in the name [of the Lord]. This prayer uttered in faith will reclaim the one who is ill, and the Lord will restore him to health . . . "

In 1941 Jesus appeared to Sister Mary of the Holy Trinity and told her: "Believe Me, it is with trials that I send My greatest graces."

One person who has received many such graces was Pat McCarthy, a woman whose burdens have been lightened by her God-given sense of humor.

When Pat, her husband and five children were living in St. Louis in 1967, she became ill one Friday afternoon while shopping with her mother.

"Everything hurts and aches, Mom," she admitted. But the discomfort faded and she quickly overlooked the problem.

But by Sunday evening, Pat was in such pain and misery that her husband had to rush her to the Emergency Room of their nearest hospital.

"Your wife's in serious trouble," the doctor began. "Besides having a severe case of Asian Flu, she has double pneumonia and pleurisy. Even worse than that, Pat hasn't got one single white cell left in her body to fight the infections. I don't see how she can possibly make it!"

PAT: For several days, I was in and out of consciousness as the staff fought to save my life. Finally, I began to show signs of improvement.

After several days, I regained enough strength to go home. Eventually, the time came for my checkup. As I sat in my doctor's office, I worried he had bad news because he kept looking at me and shaking his head.

"It's a miracle you survived this thing, Pat. A real miracle!"

But inside, Pat already knew that, and she thanked God!

GOING FIFTY-FIFTY

by
Bob Wensing

Today I'm a happy, retired podiatrist, but in 1983 I was diagnosed as having bladder cancer. Given less than a fifty-fifty chance of recovery, I joined my family, friends and fellow worshippers of the Adoration Chapel in asking God to place his healing hands upon me.

Quite awhile later, after the diseased organ had been removed, with a follow-up of radiation treatments and many days of convalescence, the physician told me that I was fine.

But the following Thanksgiving, while golfing with my son in Chicago, I experienced pain in my lower right back. What's going on now? I wondered.

Back home, new tests indicated the presence of a large five-pound tumor in the space where my bladder had once been. A second surgery and biopsy confirmed that the mass was cancerous.

"Amazingly, the news is good in that, unlike normal cancers that spread because they're not confined, your tumor is completely encapsulated. None of the cells have escaped," my physician told me. "Somebody up there likes you!"

Our entire family offered up prayers of praise and thanksgiving to that "Somebody." But our relief only lasted until the Fourth of July when I came face-to-face with another potentially-fatal ailment that sent me back for medical help. The doctors sent me immediately to Mayo's Clinic.

There, tests revealed a dangerous and massive abdominal infection.

"I'm sorry, but we can't promise you anything, Bob. In fact, your chances of making it are very slight," the doctor admitted.

Surprisingly, at that instant I felt a surge of inner strength. "Well, Doc," I remembered telling the physician. "You do your job and let God do His! Then we'll both see what happens."

As faith would have it, I lived happily ever after, despite another serious problem I encountered because I had overdosed during my radiation treatments. Then, I had a major bout with osteomiolitis, a serious bone infection that I literally prayed my way through—and won.

Not only did the Lord allow me to outwit two cancers, a deadly abdominal infection that sent my weight from 228 to 140 pounds, and another serious infection, I astounded my doctor at Mayo's when I walked into his office, many pounds regained, for my follow-up examination.

"I can't believe you're the same man," the doctor said.

I smiled. "You see how it is," I replied. "You did your part and God did His!"

OUR LADY'S A MOTHER, TOO!

by

Patricia (Pat) Middendorf

Shortly after the birth of my second daughter, I discovered a lump in my breast. Since my dear mother-in-law was fighting her own battle with breast cancer, she was quick to give me a small metal bottle containing holy water from the shrine at Lourdes. She believed that if I used the water, Our Lady would intercede with her son, Jesus Christ, and I would be healed.

But, being a recent convert to Catholicism, it was difficult for me to place my faith in such things. So, I thanked her, and put the container away on a bathroom shelf. Fortunately, the lump was removed and proved to be benign.

Then, five years later, after my son was born, another large lump appeared in approximately the same area. I prayed and again, the lump was removed. No malignancy, Thank God!

But the surgeon had surprising news for me. "The wall of your chest is covered with many small tumors, tumors that are likely to enlarge and cause problems for you in the future," he said.

Now I was scared, really scared. I was still a young woman with four children who were counting on me. I remembered the small metal bottle of holy water that had been sitting on my bathroom shelf for over five years. I thought about the sweet woman who had given it to me shortly before she lost her fight against cancer. I had to do something, something besides worry. So I turned to the Blessed Virgin Mary, and trusted that she would talk to her Son.

Everyday for several weeks, I applied the Lourdes water across the area of the tumors while saying an Our Father, a Hail Mary and a Glory Be. Mary had become my sustaining strength during that time.

Several weeks later when I went to the doctor for my scheduled checkup, the physician checked out the area of my chest wall, not once but twice. There was a look of bewilderment on his face.

"Pat, I don't understand what could have happened, but every one of your cysts has disappeared," he said.

Ever since that time, I have been so grateful to Our Lord and the Blessed Virgin for their wonderful favor. Mary understood my fear. After all, Our Lady's A Mother, Too!

GOD'S HEALING HANDS

by

Ida "Burny" Smith

Everyone takes good health for granted, but when something comes along that literally knocks you off your feet, you turn to prayer as well as medication.

Yes, until I reached the age of forty I thought that rheumatoid arthritis was something that only others and older people got—not me!

But by the age of forty-two, I had learned to live with its pain. Inflamed, deteriorating joints made the simplest tasks difficult to do, like dressing myself and combing my hair. Of course, some days were better than others, but on those other days, the pain was often excruciating.

Still, the Lord kept my spirits up by strengthening my sense of humor. "I may have arthritis, but it doesn't have me!" I'd assure those around me with a grin.

Despite many reconstructive surgeries, I kept going through exercises and stretching. Braces, gadgets, special shoes, splints and wheelchairs filled my house and my life, as did trips to Hot Springs, Desert Springs and the Mayo Clinic where I had treatments. To ease the pain, we spent our winters in Las Vegas. Still the disease continued to involve additional joints.

Every night my husband and I prayed for my healing. Even after twenty-five years of living with the arthritis, we had faith that one day something very special would happen.

In November 1995 I attended church services and, as usual, I could hardly walk. Our pastor noticed my pain and suggested group prayer on my behalf. Although this wasn't something our members did very often, the Lord seemed to be leading them that day.

The pastor asked that I bow my head and close my eyes while he and five others prayed for my healing. For several minutes they asked God to rid me of my disabling disease.

Immediately afterwards, I cannot say that I felt any different, but my belief in God's power had been strengthened. I went home.

The next morning I got up, and for the first time in twenty-five years, I wasn't stiff or sore. It usually took me two hours just to get out of bed and get going in the morning. But, here I was, moving around with no difficulty.

It took several days for me to realize what had happened. Naturally, I was afraid the stiffness and pain would return, but it didn't! My husband, who had been my pillar of support, rejoiced with me and said, "Praise the Lord for this miracle!"

Yes, a miracle had happened. When I returned to Mayos in May, my doctor told me I looked well, and after numerous tests, she said I seemed to be fine. There was a look of amazement on her face as she scribbled on her medical notes, "She says she was cured by prayer."

Indeed, I was, and today I'm physically fit. I exercise a lot and am off all medication. Once again I'm able to enjoy life—thanks to God's Healing Hands!

A MIRACLE FOR D.J.

by
Marcella Davis

Eleven years ago when my daughter Marla and her husband Donnie presented me with a beautiful grandson, D.J., I was a very happy and proud grandmother. But eight months later, at the time when our daughter Joy was getting married, D.J. became ill, causing Marla to miss her sister's wedding reception in order to take the sick baby to the Emergency Room for treatment.

Two days later, when there was no improvement, Marla and D.J. visited the doctor's office, four days in a row, where he received penicillin shots and treatments for his breathing. Then, by Saturday, when the little boy was feeling better, we took him to Singspiration at our church to offer up prayers of thanksgiving.

But the next morning, D.J. was sick again and was placed under the care of his physician who treated him for tracheal bronchitis. The child vomited every half hour, and the doctor assured us this was the body's way of ridding itself of mucus buildup.

When I stopped at Marla's house the following day, I was quite concerned about my grandbaby. Something inside was telling me to do more, and the minute I saw D.J., I knew I had to voice my opinion. The child couldn't even hold his head up.

"D.J. should be in the hospital," I insisted to both Marla and the doctor, who I called on the phone a short time later. That inner voice kept prompting me to speak up for a little boy who wasn't getting better. I really don't remember what I said but, to humor me more than anything else, the physician finally admitted my grandson to Blessing Hospital. There, he was hooked up to an IV and sent to X-ray where a shadow was detected. A CAT scan was ordered.

"Your son has a large tumor, the size of his heart, and it's compressed between the heart and his spine," the doctor told Marla and Donnie in his office. "We're taking him to Springfield."

The news was devastating. After an immediate call to my friends at church who set the prayer chain in motion, I phoned our family members. While I prayed quietly for the little boy's healing, other patients on the floor, their family members and several nurses offered to pray. But it wasn't until the nurse who escorted us to our car said, "I'll pray for you!" that I knew, but did not want to admit, just how serious the situation really was. Still, I begged God for a miracle.

But during the next several days in Springfield, we faced that seriousness. When the surgeon, a cancer specialist, told us what to expect, he seemed to be preparing us for the worst, especially when he explained how the broviac catheter is used for chemotherapy, should there be a malignancy.

"But if I don't operate, your son could die within three months. The tumor is already curving around his backbone and in between his ribs, which means that the mass is attaching itself to everything around it. Still, there's always a chance that the tumor is benign, so don't give up hope!"

And we didn't. We prayed even harder, if that was possible. Marla and I went to the chapel, but it was crowded so we sat outside. As we talked, I noticed my daughter's great faith and strength.

"D.J.'s going to be all right, Mom," Marla insisted. "Don't worry! I know there's a reason that this is happening; I just don't know what it is right now. But God's going to take care of everything."

I felt as if our roles had been reversed. I wanted to be there for my daughter, and here she was, lifting ME up.

At four a.m. the next morning, the day of surgery, my husband joined us at the hospital. Kenneth had always been there when I needed him, and I certainly needed him then.

Around 7:30 a.m., D.J. received his shot prior to the operation. He quickly fell asleep, and Marla sat rocking him. It was then that she asked us to form a circle around her chair so we could pray that God's will be done.

As we closed our prayers, Marla said, "Mom, I know that God is with D.J. because he's sleeping now." But only seconds later, my grandson popped his little head up from his mother's shoulder and smiled one of his biggest smiles ever. From that moment on, I knew the Lord was in control and that our little boy would be all right.

The six-hour operation seemed more like an eternity. When the surgeon finally came in to see us, he said that everything had gone better than expected. "Unfortunately, the tumor was malignant, a neuroblastoma," he told us. "But I believe we got it all, and D.J. is doing well, considering that the growth had already attached itself to everything except his heart."

When we were finally able to see my grandson in I.C.U., there was a broviac catheter (a drainage tube) attached to his small body, and there was an IV in both his neck and his foot. But to our surprise, the little boy was crawling all over his crib, refusing to stay under his oxygen tent, even though the nurse was trying to give him morphine for pain.

Three days later when the morphine had worn off, D.J. was on his road to recovery. That afternoon Marla was just hanging up the phone when she looked at me and said, "a lady in our prayer chain has received a sign from God that D.J. will be healed."

"But you know what the doctor said, Marla," I reminded my daughter. "I have no doubts that God will heal him, but D.J. will probably still have to take chemotherapy treatments."

Marla put both of her hands on my shoulders and shook me, saying, "I believe in God's healing power, and I want you to believe it with me."

"Okay, honey. I believe it!" I replied. "I believe that God will provide A Miracle For D.J."

Even though my grandson had to endure a bone marrow harvest in the event marrow was ever needed, God saw to it that there was no need to surgically remove the broviac catheter. When a nurse checked beneath the bandage, she found it completely out of his body, laying on his shoulder. When the doctor was called and informed about it, the physician said, "I see no need for either the catheter—or chemotherapy."

Yes, Jesus is alive and well! Today, this once-sick little boy is almost eleven years old—he is happy, healthy and a very active young person who is ever thankful that God healed him.

Praise you Lord!

~ CHAPTER 9 ~

Visions of Angels

"See, I am sending an angel before you, to guard you on the way and bring you to the place I have prepared. Be attentive to him and heed his voice . . . "

(Exodus 23:20–21)

As you will see in these beautiful stories of celestial apparitions, angels do make themselves visible to persons being helped or blessed. However, one type of angelic intervention that failed to appear as a story for this book are incidents where angels are seen only by onlookers.

An excellent example of this can be found in Billy Graham's, Angels: God's Secret Agents. (Refer to "Angel of Atlantis", Chapter 12) Hostile island natives stopped in their attack on a missionary complex when they saw powerful winged warriors surrounding and protecting the helpless compound. The missionaries inside failed to see their saving angels.

In other books on angels there are stories in which gangs who planned to harm someone, later revealed that they changed their minds after "seeing a huge man in a white suit standing behind a prospective victim!" or after they "saw two big boyfriends, one walking on either side, accompanying their young woman victim down a darkened street."

There are amazing stories in which blond-haired messengers were seen seated either beside or behind those being saved in cars, trucks and airplanes.

Whether angels are seen or unseen, their presence is unmistakable. Enter now our chapter by chapter countdown to, what we trust will be, a new or renewed belief that angels are always with us. It is only at times that they choose to be visible.

"You will receive all that you pray for provided you have faith."

(Mt. 21:22)

THE ANGELS OF O.L.A.

(As Told By The Three Women Who Saw Them)

Part 1: *by Billie Brod*

Teenagers need love, and the Great River T.E.C. (Teens Encounter Christ) is a spiritual retreat weekend for this age group that helps to meet this need.

It was in March 1988 (on T.E.C. #121) that I served on the adult team, along with my husband Bob, my grown daughter Bonnie and her friend, Peg Markle. The girls were to play guitar for the weekend where we came to know fifty very special young people. We also experienced something one can only imagine. But wait, I'm getting ahead of myself.

First, let me tell you that the week leading up to this TEC had been obstacle-filled, as usually happens before any really Christ-filled weekend.

Since TEC fell on Palm Sunday weekend, recruiting a Spiritual Director was almost impossible. But, finally, one priest consented.

Then, two weeks prior to the retreat, he cancelled, and in a panic, I telephoned every priest I knew. When no one could help, I turned to God, strangers and the Yellow Pages. Fortunately, St. Brigid's Church at Liberty was listed at the top of the page and Fr. Bill Overmann, a Franciscan, said "Yes!" immediately.

Father Overmann was like a gift from God, a regular Jesus-figure to teenager and adult alike. Everybody loved him.

The TEC weekend was overwhelming. God's presence filled the hallways, rooms (including those used for sleeping) and the chapel. That presence grew stronger as the TECites drew closer and closer to their Savior.

It was Monday afternoon at four o'clock when everyone was assembled in the Chapel for the closing liturgy of the Mass. It was quiet and heads were bowed in prayer. Imagine, fifty teens being silent at one time. Amazing!

As I sat there in that grace-filled moment, meditating on the crucifix on the far marblelike wall, I could almost feel static in the air, as if it were charged with the Holy Spirit.

Suddenly, I became aware of light filtering in from somewhere above me. I looked up.

There, suspended in mid-air over the altar, glistened an oval of such concentrated raw energy and brilliance that I could scarcely look at it. Only the faintest outline of wings and a centralized patch of pure white was visible among the multitude of long strobe-like bolts of lightning that seemed to explode outward from the center of the pulsating vision.

I was mesmerized as my mind drank in the spectacle. It's an angel, I thought to myself joyfully as I stared at the vision, lost in its mysterious and awesome glory. From its source flowed love, peace and pure happiness to the extent that I became oblivious to anyone and anything around me.

Seconds later, the angelic light faded.

I turned to look over my shoulder at those around and behind me. Had they, too, witnessed the sight? Most people prayed silently, but one teen exclaimed, "I feel as if I'm completely filled with God!"

I glanced at the other side of the chapel where Bonnie and Peg were waiting to accompany us on their guitars. My daughter was signaling me with her arms and pointing to something, gesturing toward the same spot where I had seen the brilliant angel. Peg was smiling, and I assumed they had witnessed the same glorious apparition.

Later, my husband Bob told me that he had seen the bright light, but since he was praying and thought someone had taken a flash photo, he didn't look up.

Ever since that wonderful day I have thanked God for giving me the privilege of meeting one of his heavenly messengers. From photos I've seen on video and in books, I can identify the brilliant oval of light as being one of the Lord's beautiful Thrones angels. (See the example on cover)

"Sing to the Lord with Thanksgiving; sing Praise with the harp of our God." (Ps. 147:7)

Part 2: *by Bonnie Brod-Stickney*

Like my mother, Billie Brod, I was inspired by the 1988 TEC weekend. Just as Mass was about to begin, Peg and I stood on the right side of the chapel, a bit away from the others since we were to provide the music.

At first, I became aware of the flashing light in my peripheral vision. Then, as I focused on the illumination I glanced toward the stained-glass windows to see if light was filtering in from that direction. It wasn't! The beautiful light was its own source and I realized we were in the presence of an angel.

As the concentrated area of brilliance continued to pulsate with electrical energy, I was so excited that I could hardly stand still. An inner joy was actually taking my breath away, and I felt God's love pouring into me through the rays of his magnificent angel.

I looked sideways at Peg. From the smile on her face, I assumed that she, too, had been caught up in the same vision.

Then the light faded.

Mom turned around and looked our way with excitement written all over her face. I pointed toward the marble wall to let her know that we had shared the same heavenly visitor.

Part 3: *by Peg Markle*

(Note—Billie and Bonnie assumed that Peg had witnessed the same angel they had seen just prior to the Liturgy. However, when I asked Peg about the specific time and angel, we discovered some interesting developments in this trilogy)

Bonnie and I were musicians for T.E.C. #121 at O.L.A. when she and I experienced the appearance of two angels, one in the chapel and another one who appeared in our room the night before. But we'll tell you about that later.

Apparently, I didn't see the same angel that Bonnie and her mother, Billie, saw. It was during the Mass, just before the Communion, when our group was gathered around the altar that I saw a glittering circle of light that danced around, first on the dark green marble of the wall and then on the ceiling behind the altar.

After glancing at the stained-glass windows to see if sun rays might be creating the illusion and discovering there was nothing to see, I realized that these strobe-like flashes of light were not of this world. An angel had come to the Chapel Of Our Lady of Angels!

I watched, staring in awe as the bright circle move around, disappearing and reappearing, glittering and flashing like extended flashes from a flashbulb. Then, the light disappeared.

In looking back, I believe my visitor was very different from the angel who appeared to Bonnie and Billie. Their vision remained steady while mine moved around, almost playfully. Perhaps this happened because of what happened to Bonnie and I the previous night in our room. See what you think!

NIGHT LIGHTS

by
Bonnie Brod-Stickney
Peg Markle

Peg: It was Sunday night. Actually, it was two a.m. on Monday morning. Bonnie and I were in our beds on opposite walls of our compact sleeping quarters.

Bonnie: The lights were out and it was really dark. Still, our eyes were wide open as we talked about many things, among them how the Holy Spirit had moved among the TECites that day.

Peg: Suddenly, a bright circle of light appeared where the door would be. It was waist-high and it glistened as it moved around.

Bonnie: By now, the light had jumped to the wall above my bed, like some glittering spotlight that liked to wander.

Peg: "Did you see that?" I asked Bonnie, who was checking the window to see if the light could be a reflection. No! Everything in the room, including the slot beneath the door, was pitch black.

Bonnie: I knew something amazing was taking place because I remember yelling, "It's an angel, Peg!"

Peg: All of a sudden, I felt very afraid and I pulled the covers securely over my head. I was trembling.

Bonnie: But I was in total awe of what I was witnessing. A heavenly circle of light was moving about our room. It seemed to bounce from wall to wall, shimmering. "It's beautiful!" I told Peg, who was still hiding.

Peg: It was then, when Bonnie told me, "Peg, it's on the wall behind you!" that I cried out in a muffled tone from beneath my bedding, "I don't want to look! Turn on the light!"

Bonnie: I knew my roommate was scared, and I don't remember exactly if I started to get out of bed or what, but the angelic night light vanished.

Peg: And with it, my fears disappeared. I threw the covers back and after turning on the lights, Bonnie and I squealed like children. In the moments that followed, we laughed, hugged and jumped, up and down, first—on the floor and then on the beds. On the floor again, and then, we used the beds as trampolines again.

Bonnie: What joy! What exhilaration! We were children praising God for our bright night-light visitor.

Peg: As soon as we quieted down, Bonnie told me everything she knew about angels, which was considerable. I was so excited, I cried out, "Oh, please, come back, Angel. I'm not afraid now. Please, come back!"

But he didn't—not then, anyhow!

Instead, the angel made Peg wait until the following day before he reappeared for a repeat performance in the Chapel of O.L.A.—Our Lady of Angels!

DOG'S BEST FRIEND

by

Sharon Zehnle

As "empty nesters" my husband and I are now ruled by a twenty pound ball of fluff, our beloved Lhasa Apso named Bixby. Neither of us grew up with anything but outside dogs, so we had no idea that you could form such a close relationship with a pet. What a pleasant surprise! She really has become a member of the family.

When Bixby was about six months old, she enjoyed sitting on our front porch at the end of a long tether. This gave her enough freedom to roll in the grass, check out the driveway or simply nap on the welcome mat in the warm sun.

One spring evening when she was on this porch, or so I thought, I gently eased our car back out of the garage, careful to clear the door on one side and the lawnmower on the other. I was almost halfway out of the door when, suddenly, the car stopped moving. It simply stopped! The engine was still running and I had not stepped on the brakes, but even in those few moments of wondering what had happened and why—I thought of Bixby.

Frantically, I shifted gears into "park", and jumped from the vehicle, fearful of what I might see beneath the heavy frame.

"Bixby!" I screamed when I noticed that her chain led directly to and under the center of the car. Terrified, I fell to my knees.

Pressing my shoulder and ear against the driveway, I was able to see only one thing at the opposite side, a quivering ball of fur. Our puppy was safe, but petrified with fear in her eyes, and her chain pulled as tight as it would go.

I raced around to the other side of the car, scooped Bixby up into my arms and, while comforting her with my heart racing, I praised and thanked God for protecting my "baby."

But wait! This isn't the end of the story.

Within minutes and still a bit rattled, I continued on my way to my Wednesday prayer meeting. Each week part of our gathering includes sharing what God has done in our lives since we last met. I was eager to tell Bixby's story.

But as I began to share and mentioned my car's unexplained stop, a vision suddenly came to my "mind's eye" which allowed me to see the real reason Bixby hadn't been killed that night.

In the flashback I saw what I had not been able to see earlier—an angel stretched out on his side lying directly behind the front wheels of my car. The heavenly being was very tall and slim with extremely long folded wings that protruded through his long flowing, purplish-white gown. He had purposely positioned himself as a speed bump to allow our precious puppy to cross safely behind him.

As the reality of the vision began to assimilate inside my head, my friends waited. I tingled with excitement, thinking that an angel had been within touching distance of me that evening. Finally, I was able to share this marvelous new data, of Bixby's real rescuer. What rejoicing then!

Everyone agreed that, sometimes—an Angel is a Dog's Best Friend!

Looking back in time, I've come to appreciate this unusual intervention more and more. I believe the sight of the Angel lying behind the front wheels was withheld from me because the mission was over and the Angel had already left when I dropped to my knees. However, God, in His goodness, allowed me to visualize the angel in action to answer my question of what stopped my car.

Since that time, gift shops around the world abound with tall, skinny figures of Santas, angels and other crafts. Could others have been visited by angels such as Bixby's to inspire such figure duplication?

And isn't it wonderful that God shows such concern for our animal friends that he protects them, too? St. Martin de Porres of Lima, Peru reportedly raised a dog from the dead, while St. John Bosco, Founder of the Society of St. Francis de Sales, brought a dead ox and a hen back to life. Were these pets as well?

NANNIES FROM HEAVEN

by
Carolyn Witsken

"Father, Lord of heaven and earth, to you I offer praise; for what you have hidden from the learned and the clever you have revealed to the merest children." (Mt. 11:25)

It was nearly ten years into our married life when the Lord blessed us with our first daughter, and what a blessing it was! This long-awaited child was a beautiful baby with black kinky hair, almond-shaped eyes and otherwise, perfect, except for her inherited characteristic of limp hanging little toes.

How I had prayed and begged God for this child. And here I was holding her in my arms. To be quite honest, I was a bit overwhelmed with all the ramifications of her care, so I began to pray daily for the angels to watch over her, a prayer process that continued for all these 34 years, and one that now includes her husband and children.

At "bad dream" times, I always reassured her that she need never fear; that God loved her and would send His angels to watch over her.

One night when she was almost four years old, I remember going into her bedroom to check on her and her baby sister. Little sister was in her crib sound asleep, but my firstborn was quite awake, seated at the foot of her bed where she looked intently out her window.

"What are you doing? How come you're still awake?" I asked her. The little curly head looked up and replied, "I'm just watching the angels!"

"Really?" I exclaimed, taken aback by the response. "Where are they? And with that, I bent over and peered through the glass.

"They're out there by the roof of the garage," the child replied, quite matter-of-factly.

Our garage was only about eight feet from her window, so my next question was, "What are the angels doing?"

With a deep sigh, the four-year-old said, "Oh, they're mostly just flying around out there watching me!"

"Well, then, why don't you climb back in bed and go to sleep?" I suggested, confused and amused when I saw nothing.

Obediently, the small figure wiggled beneath the covers, and we said her prayers again.

That was several years ago. This little girl grew up, married and now has several children of her own. I often think about her telling me of angels around the garage roof. Recently I made a point to ask her about it, to see what she remembered of the incident.

"Did you really see angels that night?" I asked.

"Yes, I did!" she responded, without hesitation. "In fact, that wasn't the only night they were there. I remember seeing them several other nights as well."

I decided to delve a bit deeper.

"What did the angels look like?"

The young woman thought a bit. "It's been a while, but I can still see them, probably four small cherub-type angels in white whispy gowns—all floating around in a circle over one corner of the garage roof as they watched me. They may have had wings, but I'm not sure of that. It's been awhile, you know."

"Did you ever see angels at either of the other two houses in which we lived?" I questioned.

"No! After we left the house on Madison Street, I never saw them again."

Since our conversation, I've thought about possible explanations. Could there have been some light reflections? But as I recall, no one had garage lights on either the inside or outside, and the street lights were farther down on the corner, which put them at the front side of our house. Then I wondered if the fact that it was so dark actually made it possible for her to see them.

No matter what, I believe angels still surround this daughter, as well as the others in my family, because I pray daily that the Lord will send them to protect my loved ones.

My eldest daughter now has a five-year-old son who was born too soon and weighed a mere one pound and a half ounce. But he had angels protecting him from the start, and now, right on schedule, he's entering kindergarten this fall. Even when he was in his incubator, I used to talk to him and tell him Grandma only weighed a pound more (even before today's technology), and that he was going to be okay. After all, he had help, too, from those round-the-clock Nannies From Heaven.

It should not be surprising that God allows special favors for children. After all, Jesus Christ said, "I assure you, unless you change and become like little children, you will not enter the kingdom of God. Whoever makes himself lowly, becoming like this child, is of greatest importance in that heavenly reign." (Mt. 18:3–4)

And in Mt. 18:10 He says, "See that you never despise one of these little ones. I assure you, their angels in heaven constantly behold my heavenly Father's face."

In Deuteronomy 5 the Ten Commandments of the Lord are laid out. Then, in Deuteronomy 6:1 we read, "These then are the commandments, the statutes and decrees which the LORD, your God, has ordered that you be taught to observe . . . " And in Deuteronomy 6:5–9, "Therefore, you shall love the LORD, your God, with all your heart, and with all your soul, and with all your strength. Take to heart these words which I enjoin you today. Drill them into your children. Speak of them at home and abroad, whether you are busy or at rest. Bind them at your wrist as a sign and let them be as a pendant on your forehead. Write them on the doorposts of your houses and on your gates."

~ Chapter 10 ~

Of God, Angels and Man

In May 1996 the small town of Mount Washington, Kentucky was devastated by a tornado. The next morning as I watched the TV news, my attention was drawn to the picture of a single wall that remained standing in the midst of an area otherwise leveled by the twister. There, above the rubble, and miraculously unscathed on that lonely wall, a large crucifix hung in place, despite the ferocity of winds that must have grabbed at it as they wracked the town of five thousand. I could only imagine the torrent of prayers that must have swirled heavenward that night along with the destructive funnel that injured very few of the residents.

As I stared at the crucifix, I tried to visualize the bevy of angels that must have worked overtime to help the people of Mount Washington.

To date, the presence of angels has never been proven in a laboratory by human beings, who seem to require proof of everything. Jesus Christ Himself must have sighed when he said, "Unless you people see signs and wonders, you do not believe." (John 4:48)

But, believe, you will, once God personally intervenes in your life with a miracle. You'll find yourself asking God, "Why me, Lord? Why choose me?" Even Vicka Ivankovic, one of the visionaries at Medjugorje, asked the Blessed Mother, "Why did you choose me?" Our Lady replied, "I do not always pick the best."

But, as God's children, we ARE His best, and He has been helping us ever since Paradise was lost to us. In the Old Testament, God performed an abundance of miracles, while Jesus Christ, besides sacrificing Himself for us on the Cross to reopen the gates of Heaven, performed a multitude of miracles in the New Testament. Of course, God still performs wonders today! " . . . know that I am with you always, until the end of the world." (Mt. 28:20)

And in Acts 2:17 Jesus said (through Luke), "It shall come to pass in the last days, says God, that I will pour out a portion of my spirit on all mankind; Your sons and daughters will prophesy, your young men will see visions and your old men shall dream dreams."

Yes, God is always with us as are his angels, whether we see them or not. But as much as they want to help us, these Miracle Makers never violate our free wills. Until we are able to set that free will aside and invite these heavenly visitors into our space, they are unable to act. Also, should we foolishly break the law of man or purposely put ourselves in harm's way, we can hardly expect God or the angels to protect us. But remember, your angel is always awaiting your call for assistance.

In Eileen Elias Freeman's book, *Touched by Angels,* she tells us what angels would say to us if they had the chance:

"We are not the beginning and end of all things. We are creatures, just as you are. Don't get trapped into thinking we make plans for you, that we discuss your futures, that we can bring you untold wealth and perfect health and long life if you push the right buttons.

We don't do any of those things, and we don't want you to ask us to do them. Those kind of things are God's province, not ours. When we work for your benefit from our dimension, we do so because God created us to do this. When you see or hear or sense us in yours, it is because we have been sent by the One who sends us. We have no messages of our own; every single one of them comes from God. We have no personal grace to give you, no private messages of enlightenment. They come from God.

Please don't be blinded by our light. Yes, it's glorious and wonderful, but it's just our nature to be that way. We find your combination of matter and mind and spirit just as glorious a manifestation of God's infinite diversity, as wonderful as you find us. Our light and yours stem from the same Source. We are created beings. We did not make ourselves. We are servants, tutors, guides. It is the way we are; we love it that way.

Yes, there are many differences between our races. We have seen your world spun out of the dust of the solar system. At God's command, we helped to spin it. We have seen you grow up on this planet. We have never died, nor will we. We do not rebel against our natures as you do, at least not anymore. We do not age or know ill health. But should you thank us for this? Should you make offerings to us? No. We are just being true to our natures. Be true to yours—grow, love, learn wisdom, unite body, soul and mind. This is all we ask, and it is not even we who ask it; it is God who asks."

Ah, yes, the Angels! Those gentle stirrings of wind, feathers rubbing, one against the other, are our true and faithful friends. As such they deserve our time, attention and a "thank you", every once in a while or more. They also deserve a little recognition at bedtime to thank them for their protective gaze.

I remember the words I said as a child, "Angel of God, my guardian dear. To whom his love commits me here. Ever this day be at my side, to light and guard, to rule and guide. Amen"

Or you might enjoy using the following as a prayer or a poem:

Angel standing at my shoulder,
hovering above my head,
wrap me in your wings and shield me,
sit beside me on my bed.

Angel walking in my shadow,
helping me when things go wrong,
shelter me secure and hide me
from the darkness all day long.

Angel speaking through my conscience,
be my confidant and friend,
hold me close and one day lead me
into Heaven at life's end.

~ CHAPTER 11 ~

Heaven Help Our Highways!

As everyone knows, traveling America's highways can be a delightful or a frightful experience, simply because human beings control powerful machines that are capable of killing. Hence the reason that the Miracle Makers must intervene so often everyday on concrete, blacktop and gravel.

This book would not be complete without stories that deal with paths of public transportation. One example involves a dirt road that winds through the steamy Brazilian jungle. Most of us can relate to, at least, one incident in which some intervention or a Blessed Coincidence took place on a highway; perhaps, we were the one saved.

In other works about angels, there are awesome accounts of unbelievable accidents in which the occupants of vehicles have walked away from the scene, literally unscathed. There are stories of angels who have taken on assumed human bodies in order to physically, and with the greatest of ease, lift stalled cars from railroad tracks as the train approached. Angels have been seen in the cockpits of airplanes, flying the aircraft, when the pilot was incapacitated.

Many years ago when our family was on vacation in Arizona, I was driving our car on a dual, six-lane and undivided highway, three lanes going in either direction. I must have drifted close to the center line that divided the lanes because, suddenly, I saw a car coming from the opposite direction that seemed to be headed for our left headlight. Gripping the wheel, I screamed, halfway closed my eyes and counted on God to save me.

I waited for the impact, the crunch of metal! There was no way we could avoid a collision.

But nothing happened. From the corner of my eye, I saw a passing meteor—the other vehicle that zipped past my open window as a blurred streak of light.

By now, my eyes were open, wide open, and my family was still intact. I was trembling, but thanking God for saving us. Our two vehicles passed so close to each other that every door handle and mirror should have been torn off. Had an angel come between our vehicles that day?

It would be easy to say, "Boy, were we ever lucky!" But luck has nothing to do with miracles, and miracles have everything to do with God.

Everytime we buckle up, it would be wise to invite God to accompany us and surround us with His angels. Driving responsibly is imperative, but if danger ever presents its ugly head, the Lord and His troopers (the Blessed Mother and the angels) are always on duty and ready to spring into action.

> "For to his angels he has given command about you, that they shall guard you in all their ways. Upon their hands they shall bear you up, lest you dash your foot upon a stone." (Ps. 91:11)

LUMBERJACKS AND ANGEL WINGS

by
Rita Goerlich

"For to his angels he has given a command about you, that they guard you in all your ways . . . " I prayed the 91st Psalm along with my husband Joe and our son, Allan.

"And, Jesus, remember to place an angel at each corner of our car," I added as I closed the vehicle's door. Joe was starting the engine while 18-year-old Allan made himself comfortable in the back seat. Our Montana vacation was over and it was time to return to Illinois.

There was an irridescent glow of dawn that lay across the eastbound lane ahead of us as my husband pulled onto the highway. We settled back, confident that angels were watching over us.

Since the road handled two-way traffic, Joe soon discovered that it was easier and more relaxing not to pass, especially after several large logging trucks entered the traffic pattern. Before long, our 1984 Pontiac was stationed behind one of the big rigs.

For a time, I tried to appear at ease as I surveyed the quiet countryside. Finally, I just had to clear my throat. "This makes me nervous. Following a big pile of naked trees down a winding highway isn't my idea of a smart thing to do."

Joe's laugh was meant to be reassuring. "Those heavy chains are strong enough to hold those logs in place, Rita. Don't worry; lumberjacks know what they're doing."

As much as I wanted to believe my husband, I could feel my hands trembling. Something was wrong. "I'm sorry, Joe, but can't we pass this truck, please?" I pleaded. Even though our car seemed to be a safe distance behind the logger, I felt terribly uncomfortable.

Then, just ahead of us, we could see an overpass that stretched across both lanes of traffic. When the load of logs on the flatbed in front of us attempted to clear the structure, the top log slammed, face on, into the cement surface. We could only watch in horror as chains snapped and flew off to both sides of the unit. Instantly, the huge log became a lethal projectile from the force exerted upon it when it rammed the overpass. It was airborne and sailing directly back toward us. I knew there were vehicles behind us, and others were headed west on the left side of the road.

"Jesus, help us!" Joe and I cried out, the only words time allowed. The tree trunk had taken deadly aim at us, like some tremendous, powerful battering ram that was about to demolish our car.

At that point, I began seeing things in slow motion. My only thought was that, because my husband and I were in the front seat, we were about to die. Please don't take Allan, I thought in prayer to God as Joe pushed the brake pedal to the floorboard. The log was closing in on us fast. We were its target.

Then, suddenly, we stared in disbelief and utter amazement as the log, despite its westward trajectory, took an unexplainable ninety-degree turn in direction, came to a halt and dropped onto the pavement. By now, the squealing tires of our Pontiac had come to a complete stop, only inches from where the log rested in a north/south position.

Tears and sighs of relief plus a "Thank You, Lord!" filled the car as other vehicles, both behind us and in the left lane, stopped because of the errant log that blocked traffic.

Almost immediately, I heard someone tapping on my window. I rolled down the glass and came face to face with a young man dressed in a blue and green checkered shirt.

"Are you all right?" he asked, his voice very calm and reassuring. After I stammered, "I guess so," the stranger simply smiled and walked away, but none of us saw exactly where he went. All of the other travelers were still seated inside their cars, waiting for someone to clear the roadway.

Before long, the truck driver returned, totally unaware of the remarkable thing that had just happened. It took several husky men, using heavy tongs and other equipment, to remove the obstruction.

By the time we finally drove beneath the infamous underpass, we were sure that nothing short of a miracle had saved us that day. We still wondered about the concerned Samaritan who appeared and disappeared so suddenly from the side of the road. How did he just happen to be standing where we stopped?

And ever since our amazing experience with Lumberjacks and Angel Wings in Montana, our family gatherings become reverently silent when someone brings up the incident of the log.

BRING THE LITTLE CHILDREN UNTO ME

by

Father Pedro (Pierre) Amen

Brazil, a country that began almost 500 years ago as a small Portugese colony, is rich in resources. It covers almost half of South America and, being on the Equator, it is always damp, hot and rainy in the northern region where I live in the town of Santarém. The entire area is one of dense jungles along the deep and wide Amazon River. As a Franciscan missionary, I serve forty communities that are located along the Trans-Amazon Highway, a dirt road that wanders through the heart of the dark jungle.

Each time I must call on one of my communities the visit is restricted to one-half day, and because there are no motels in the region, our good people open both their hearts and their homes to me.

One steamy evening in the thatched school house of one community, a group of Brazilian colonists who had recently come to this road to begin a new life, were watching slides of the life of Jesus Christ. Two seminarians, who were helping me on the road, were assisting me, and the people enjoyed seeing pictures they had never seen before.

Suddenly, a man entered through the doorway. It was Artur, one of my Catechists from a neighboring community. His face looked flushed from running.

"Come quickly, Frei Pedro. It is my daughter. She has been burned badly," he cried.

Since my jeep was the only means by which to get the child to a doctor, I asked the seminarians to continue the showing. Artur and I headed out the door.

"The doctor is many miles from here, my friend," I said. "I'll need to take extra cans of gasoline."

With the cans in place and Artur in the seat beside me, we headed for his house. His three-year-old daughter had scalded her entire arm severely when she tipped boiling coffee over and onto herself. Now, as I drove, my friend prayed, and my heart went out to the small child in Artur's arms who was screaming with pain.

It was almost an hour and a half later when our vehicle's headlights flickered once and then, went out. There was no moon, no light of any kind when the jeep stopped in the pitch black night.

"Let me get out, Frei Pedro. I will see where we are," Artur volunteered as he gently sat the child on the seat and stepped outside.

A moment later, the Catechist raised his voice, "Frei, there is some big drop-off to your side, an abyss. What will you do?"

"Get your daughter out of here!" I shouted to the man who was already opening the door. Artur reached in and grabbed the sobbing child.

"Stand aside!" I stammered, and shifted gears to put the jeep into reverse. Suddenly, I sensed a sinking feeling under my side as dirt began to give way beneath the wheels. I said a quick prayer just as the jeep turned over, sideways to my left. It was as if someone had thrown me inside a revolving electric dryer. At least two-and-one-half complete rollovers later, I was shaken but miraculously, still alive, and with full realization that I had just fallen a considerable distance. The jeep rested on its left side, and my arm was wedged against the warped door.

I was stunned, and as I laid there in the darkness, I muttered, "Thank you, Jesus. Thank you!" Nothing seemed to hurt very much so I assumed the Almighty had done a mighty good job of protecting me.

But my thoughts quickly returned to Artur and his injured little girl. I cried out to him in the darkness.

"Oh, Frei Pedro. You're alive!" he yelled back, excitedly.

"Yes, thank God!" I replied, meaning every word literally.

Artur hurried down to where I was trapped to tell me he would go for help. Taking the sobbing child with him, my friend raced from house to house in the dark, gathering colonists to aid us. Because the road was a government project, there were houses every five hundred meters, and soon my friend returned with several people by means of a side road.

From my cramped position in the damaged vehicle, I could only catch a glimpse of those who were busily picking up items that had spilled from my jeep. Items like boxes of holy pictures, crucifixes, rosaries and even a course for teaching adults to read and write, along with chalk and several pairs of reading glasses, compliments of funeral home personnel who remove them before closing caskets. Many people are now able to read and write because of these glasses.

Before long, the group managed to restore the jeep, with me inside it, to its proper upright position.It was then that I remembered the cans of gasoline that had taken that topsy-turvy ride, along with me, down the hillside and yet, had not exploded. Again, I thanked the Lord!

Normally when a vehicle rolls over, the oil will run out. But when I turned the ignition key, the engine ran perfectly. Not so, the jeep itself! It looked quite crooked and the lights still didn't work. How would we get the child to the doctor? What could we do? We had to think.

"Frei Pedro, you smoke, right?" Artur asked. "Give me the aluminum foil wrapper from your cigarette pack, please. I will make a fuse that will make contact. Then, the lights will work and lead us on our way."

Artur was right, and before long, we were on the jungle road again, just a bit worse for wear.

This time as we headed down the Trans-Amazon Highway, I sensed the Lord's abiding presence, and within fifteen minutes, we were knocking on the door of the simple wooden building that housed the doctor, hired by the government, to treat the many injuries of road workers. It was eleven o'-clock and even though he had been asleep, the physician didn't mind helping the suffering child.

"Perhaps I should treat you first, Father," the doctor said, pointing to a gash on my forehead that I didn't realize was there. Instead, I insisted he treat the little girl, which he did with many salves and bandages. Then, after patching me up, the three of us retraced the many miles to Artur's house.

By the time the sun had risen, I was on my way to the next community to be visited.

Now, everytime I see Artur and his precious daughter, I thank God, not only for intervening on my behalf that night, but for allowing the child's arm to heal blemish-free and as perfect as before the accident.

(Father Amen's missionary work is one of the charities that will benefit from book sales profits)

~ CHAPTER 12 ~

Is That You, Angel?

With the exception of God's messengers who appear to us, either in their glorified state or in assumed bodies, angels usually work undercover. This is where they do their finest work and where you most often find them looking out for your best interests. Keep your eyes open for God's special agents.

HIGH WIRE ACT

by
Sharon Kay

When I was around the age of three, my family lived in a big three-story house. I remember the wonderful porch that had a railing with sturdy crossbeams on which my older cousins used to walk and balance themselves by holding onto an overhead cornice.

One day when everyone else was downstairs playing in the backyard, I decided to try my own High Wire Act. But being small and short, I quickly toppled sideways and fell from the narrow beam, plunging headfirst, down and toward a yard that had been sectioned off with a thin wire to keep children off of the grass.

One of my cousins saw me falling. She screamed, but I don't remember anything after that. Something or someone miraculously caught me under my chin and somehow, flipped me over so that I landed flat on the ground on my stomach, instead of the knife-sharp wire.

Thanks to God or His angel, a small gash beneath my chin and a few stitches were the only injuries I sustained from my High Wire Act.

ANGEL AT THE WHEEL

by
Mary Talken

It was April 1976 when my mother was diagnosed as having cancer, and we were forced to admit her to Good Samaritan Home. It was then that she expressed her desire that the three of us—my father, my sister, Rita, and I—be with her when the end came. So, from that moment on, we prayed that God would make it possible.

The humid summer months dragged on while Daddy spent every waking hour at his terminally-ill wife's bedside. Besides visiting Mom almost every day, I cleaned Dad's house and did his grocery shopping, while Rita volunteered to sleep overnight in our mother's room when conditions warranted it.

Already Mother had deteriorated. She could no longer speak and her only communication was through her glazed-over eyes that searched our faces and the ceiling for relief. Still, her heart continued to beat, strong and steady.

By the first part of September Mom's breathing became labored and Rita began sleeping at Good Samaritan in her room. Since our brothers worked (and one lived out of town), they weren't always able to be there.

Monday, September 13th—I arrived at Dad's house at eight a.m., just as he was backing his car from the garage.

"After I clean house, I'll go to Krogers and then come by to see Mom," I promised. The Impala moved slowly away as Dad turned the corner and headed west on Holiday Drive. At 36th Street, he turned left and headed toward Good Samaritan.

Then, for some unknown reason, I changed my mind and decided to do the shopping first. Back inside my car, I drove west on the same route Dad had taken only minutes earlier. As I approached 36th Street, I flipped on my right-turn blinkers and waited for traffic to clear so I could go to Krogers.

I turned the steering wheel; at least, I tried to turn the wheel to the right, but the mechanism wouldn't budge. Again, I gripped the wheel and turned right, but the wheel column remained locked in place. Two more times I tried, but without luck.

I was frustrated. Now, what do I do? I thought as I sat, quietly thinking. Suddenly, I sensed something inside the car with me, a presence of some kind. At first, it seemed to be behind me; then it was around me, embracing me.

At the moment, another car pulled up behind mine and honked its horn. After one last futile attempt at a right turn, I flipped on my left blinkers and eased out into traffic, headed left toward Good Samaritan.

At Harrison Street making a right turn was no problem, and within minutes, I had parked the car and was opening the door of the Infirmary.

I came face-to-face with my sister who was on her way home. "What are you doing here?" she asked. "Daddy said you were cleaning this morning."

Before I could respond, we heard our father's raised voice coming down the long corridor that led to Mom's room. He could see us from where he stood on the far side of her bed.

"Hurry, girls, Hurry!" he shouted. "Your mother's dying."

Leather heels resounded off hard tile as we rushed toward Room 338. Mom's frail body reared up and down, and slammed against the clammy mattress, several times.

We paused at the doorway, filled with reverence for the moment and the realization that God had allowed us to fulfill the promise to our mother.

Rita and I entered the room and stopped in silence at the foot of her bed. We were all there together!

Then the spasms ceased and the fragrance of roses filled the air. Although I didn't actually see an angel, I sensed that one was escorting Mom's spirit away from the mortal shell that held it captive and into a glorious new life.

In 1976 I assumed it was Mother's angel that had come for me, so that I would stop Rita from leaving and we could be together. But now I'm convinced it was my own angel who held the steering wheel that day. Mother's angel would never have left her side that close to the moment of her death, the time that Satan makes every last-ditch attempt to gain control of a human soul.

ANGELS IN ATTENDANCE

by
Sharon Kay

A couple years ago when my younger sister was terminally ill, our family supported her through the long days of her sickness by praying for her and being at her bedside. During one of her hospital stays when she had taken a turn for the worse, our family was called in to say our goodbyes.

It was about 1:00 a.m. when we felt that my sister was resting well enough that we could leave to get something to eat. When we returned to the floor, I volunteered to stay with Sis until her husband came back. The others were free to go back to their motel rooms to rest.

Just as I entered the dimly-lit hospital room, I sensed the presence of many people behind me. Assuming other family members had decided to accompany me after all, I sat down on a chair at the foot of the bed, comforted by the feeling of closeness with my loved ones at hand.

But when I turned around, curious to see who was there, I discovered that I was alone in the room with my sister. Still, I felt the presence of many people around me.

A moment later, when my son Steve entered, the sensation remained the same—strong and reassuring. But the second that my brother walked in, that beautiful feeling of Angels In Attendance faded. God's ministering messengers knew my sister was being cared for, and felt free to go!

THE GREAT HOLDUP

by
Ed. J. Schumer

On Monday evenings our parish often holds a Mass of Healing where our pastor passes down the aisle, from person to person, praying over anyone who requests it. An older priest accompanies him and holds aloft the golden monstrance (the large circular receptracle in which the consecreated host is placed for people to adore).

One night our pastor stopped, for a longer period of time than usual, to pray over a young girl. The other priest, who had only recently undergone surgery, looked pale and fatigued as he struggled to hold the receptracle up for all to see.

When I asked him if I could be of service, he carefully handed me the gleaming object. How privileged I felt to hold Our Lord for my fellow parishoners.

It was two days later on Wednesday that my Drywall Company was scheduled to finish the interior of a large house. With twenty-five-foot-tall ceilings, my men and I had to set up extensive scaffolding. We shoved one end of the metal pick boards securely into 6" deep window sills while we attached the other ends of the boards onto a sturdy ladder. These pick boards were placed along three of the four sides of the house, with the longest being seventeen feet that spanned the entire front of the structure. The walkway itself was probably fifteen or more feet off the floor.

After one of my employees and I carried the material onto the walk, we began to work. (The total weight of material and men amounted to approximately 500 pounds). It was only a short time later, while I was standing a few feet away from the end of the sill, that I made a quick turn and caused the ladder to sway away from my side. I watched in horror as the end of the board on which I was standing, slipped completely out of the sill that secured it.

"Get off!" I screamed to the other man who instinctively jumped to a window sill beside him.

But I froze! My end of the pick was now completely off the sill, suspended there in space, just below sill level, and I couldn't see that anything was holding my end up.

Afraid to breath, I called down to the man who was laying brick on the fireplace. "What's holding me up?" I asked gingerly.

The workman strained his neck and replied, "Nothing!"

My heart pounded. Only a few feet separated me from the safety of the window sill. But how long could this pick board remain under me in space before it went crashing down with me along for the ride? I wondered apprehensively.

Having no choice, I inched my way in faith, closer and closer, to the sill. Finally, I jumped for it and grabbed the frame with my fingers.

I could only stare at the metal pick. Defying all laws of nature and gravity, it stayed in place, a mere two to three inches below sill level. Something invisible is holding it up, I thought.

But then, an inner voice seemed to be speaking to my mind. It was subtle, but it was very clear. And it said, "Once, you held me up. Today, I held you up!"

THE ANGEL OF ATLANTIS

by
Mary Talken

Several years ago I joined Quincy's Atlantis Club, a group of women who meet weekly from October through April and give papers on a yearly theme. In 1993 the theme was "A Book" and, since heavenly beings had always held a special place in my heart, I chose Billy Graham's book, *Angels: God's Secret Agents* for my paper.

To complement the written text, I prepared two posters, one on which various pictures of angels were displayed, and a second one that listed the nine choirs of angels, along with their celestial duties.

As a door prize, I planned to award a box of angel food cake mix. To determine the winner, I decided to paste a sticker that said, "You're An Angel!" beneath the seat of one of the chairs.

When the day of the paper arrived, I selected a chair in the middle of the room for the sticker. Then I watched as, one by one, the ladies arrived and began to fill in the chairs. By the time the meeting began, only one seat was vacant.

A late-comer entered and, instead of sitting in the last chair, she made her way around the back of the room to sit on the sofa.

"There are as many angels in this room as there a women," I began. "And everyone's angels are in attendance today. If you become sensitive to their presence, you can almost feel them."

The women's faces seemed aglow as I related stories presented by Dr. Graham. One told of Captain Eddie Rickenbacker's miraculous sea gull that suddenly perched atop his head from out of nowhere while he and a group of men were adrift on the Pacific in life boats during WWII. Rickenbacker gently killed the gull and, after dividing the tiny carcass between everyone in the boats, found it to be sufficient norishment to sustain them until they were rescued.

Graham also wrote of a deceased child who summoned a doctor from sleep to lead him through the snow to the apartment of her sick mother. There the doctor discovered the same coat hanging in the closet that the child had been wearing.

"It's been there ever since my daughter died," the mother assured him.

The evangelist also wrote of island natives who, while attempting to attack a missionary complex, backed off when they saw large numbers of angelic warriors surrounding the compound.

Finally, after explaining my posters, I finished by saying, "Now it's time to present this box of angel food cake mix. Look under your chairs for a sticker."

There was a rustle of chairs as the ladies looked, but when no one found the little piece of paper, all eyes seemed drawn to the one vacant seat in the middle of the room.

"I was sitting there when I first came in, but I moved over," one member announced. "I'll check under the chair."

When she straightened up with the sticker that had "You're An Angel!" typed on it secured to the tip of her finger, everyone was stunned.

"I think there's an angel sitting there!" President Shirley Murphy said. For an instant, the room was unusually quiet as the women stared at the vacant spot.

Finally, President Murphy broke the silence. "I've got goosebumps!" she admitted quietly.

A Blessed Coincidence? A mini-miracle God did behind our backs to support us and simply surround us with love?

A RAINBOW FROM MAMA

by

Sue Finley

My mother, Marion Reppell, was an artist, a real artist, who loved flowers and painted them in oils and every color of the rainbow.

Mom was a wonderful person. For as long as I can remember, she had been there for my dad, my brother Tom and me. She was always a pillar of strength, not only in our home, but in her church as a practicing Christian Scientist. I admired her strong convictions, and I was convinced that she was more of a Christian than I would ever be.

Over the years, I was amazed when she experienced healings through and because of her deep faith. But in 1991 Mom confronted an enemy that could not be cured and fought the battle of her life against cancer.

Her beliefs as a Christian Scientist drew the first battle lines. But, for some unknown reason, she chose to go the medical route, and within six months before her death, Mom resigned membership in her church. Though we never discussed it, I knew it hurt her, and I felt guilty, too, despite the fact that I knew I had never pushed her toward treatment.

Through all her surgeries and medical horrors, I tried to be there for her, just as she had been there for me. Daddy was an angel, and he seldom left her side. We could only watch helplessly as she suffered and became totally incapacitated.

Finally, in the wee hours of the morning of July 14, 1993 my dear mother died—in the hospital and all alone. The staff on duty somehow failed to phone my father until it was too late. I felt guilty when I received Dad's call at 8 a.m.

"We should have been there!" I said, the thought of no one being at her side almost too much to bear.

I left St. Charles immediately for the long drive along I-270 to South County. It had been two years; I was numb and stared in disbelief that Mom was finally at peace.

Since my brother Tom was coming from Kansas City by train, Dad and I made the arrangements at the funeral parlor. The minute I spied a pretty flowered casket, I knew it was the one that Mom would have chosen for herself.

Later we picked my brother up at the station, and over dinner, we shared our plans and our grief. When it was time for me to return to St. Charles, I was dreading the lonely trip by myself.

As I drove about 70 mph and all alone with my memories of Mom, tears streamed down my cheeks. I'll never share anything with you again, Mom! I thought, and I felt so terribly alone.

Suddenly, I saw something straight ahead of me, in the sky above the highway. It had not been raining, and yet, I saw the most beautiful rainbow, vibrant with every color that Mom would have brushed on a canvas of flowers. I blinked hard to squeeze the excess tears from my eyes.

As I sat behind the steering wheel, mesmerized by the sight before me, I sensed an aura of my mother's presence in front of me. Oh, what an unexpected feeling of joy!

Whether it was Mother's rainbow or not, I knew it had appeared as a sign that she was at peace, and that both of us would be okay. We could still share things through my prayers.

As a peace settled around my shoulders, I stopped crying. Slowly, the beautiful rainbow faded from sight, but not the memory of what happened on I-270 that day.

The experience would never leave. In fact, I still thank the Lord for sending to me, not only the warm feeling I carry inside me now, but for that sighting of a Rainbow From Mama!

"Then I saw another mighty angel come down from heaven wrapped in a cloud, with a rainbow about his head . . . "

(Rev. 10:1)

ANGELS TO THE RESCUE

by
Sharon Kay

One morning after church as I drove our car from the parking lot, my daughter Kellie was seated beside me in the front seat while my three-year-old son Steven occupied the seat behind me. I was totally unaware of what he was doing when he accidentally opened the back door and fell out.

Oh, I must have gone up the curb, I thought, after I sensed going over a sudden bump with the car. Then, as I pulled out onto Main Street, I noticed the back door was open and in my rear-view mirror, I saw the image of a woman who was waving her arms and signalling for me to stop.

Pulling to the curb, I parked the car and jumped out. You can imagine my amazement at seeing three-year-old Steven standing on the grass near the curb, his little arms wrapped about his chest and, obviously, in pain.

Only then did I comprehend what had just happened. I had run over my own child!

Heaven only knows how my son survived the pressure of a car going over his small body. Even though Steven was in ICU for a few days being monitored constantly for possible internal injuries, he was fine. I still shudder remembering the sight of my car's tire tracks imprinted on the back of his small white shirt. In my heart, I thanked the angels for surrounding my son and bearing most of the car's weight that day.

~ Chapter 13 ~

Angels in Disguise
(Assumed Bodies)

Sometimes angels must become visible in order to complete their earthly mission; they assume a body, a human disguise, that allows them to blend into our world, if only temporarily. As corporeal visions, they will be capable of speaking and, if necessary, physically touching us. Where these human shells come from* and where they go, once discarded, is unknown, but since several stories pertain to this specific angelic condition, we want to provide information relating to them.

Many of these encounters with visible heavenly beings have seemed so conventional, that it wasn't until much later that the people realized that they had been in the presence of an angel.

> "Do not neglect to show hospitality, for by that means some have entertained angels without knowing it."
>
> (Hebrews 13:2)

While most angels seem to be tall and larger in stature, average to shorter-sized and cherub-like angels have been reported. To recognize an angel, one must be willing and able to see them through the eyes and mind set of faith. Listening to their voice and speech pattern is most important.

1) Just as Jesus used short sentences and everyday terminology of a few but well-chosen words, so do his angels. Often they begin by asking a question, and they depend on silence and gestures to carry them through their mission.

---

*Because not all angels have wings, the body we see may actually be their angelic self, minus their usual glorious brilliance.

2) An angel's voice is usually very soft and noticeably serene. (Unless danger is involved, when it can be quite loud and authoritative.)
3) No matter what is happening around them, an angel's demeanor is usually very relaxed, even when rescuing someone in serious danger. (As with Joan Wester Anderson's son Tim in Chapter 1) Their only concern seems to be in helping the recipient of their assignment. Angels never linger, never pass the time of day with useless chit-chat, and when finished—they leave immediately!
4) Angels in assumed bodies usually appear dressed in garb most acceptable to the soul being helped. This also applies to any other items necessary for the mission.
5) Although angels in assumed bodies are said to feel some emotion, the bodies themselves do not perform any of the basic vegetative functions of human existence.

Since God's angels cannot be visible in our lives all of the time, it's up to all of us to become angels to each other in order to help these heavenly messengers in carrying out their earthly ministry.

So, be an angel to someone today and everyday! Do those random acts of kindness. Then, wait and watch as others become angelic toward you. Goodness and love are contagious, and a great place to begin is in your own home.

1. But remember, it's easy to be an angel if nobody ruffles your feathers. Even when your best efforts go unrewarded or unappreciated, hang in there. God will not be outdone in His generosity!

"KNOCK! KNOCK! WHO'S THERE?" "GOD!" "GOD WHO?" "GOD WHO LOVES YOU!"

by
Ann & Jeff Bradshaw
(Not real names)
As told by Ann

It was two years ago when we were in the process of moving our family from St. Louis to Glen Ellyn, a town west of Chicago, that we discovered how much God really loves and cares for us.

Veterans Day, November 1994—while the sale of our Missouri residence was still pending, we rejoiced in having just closed the deal on another house in Glen Ellyn. Because our children had not seen the community, Jeff and I decided to celebrate our purchase by spending the entire weekend in our new but empty home. We had brought along with us sleeping bags, lawn chairs, a card table and a television, as well as bicycles that we could use to explore and acquaint ourselves with the new surroundings. We were a family of five—my husband Jeff and I, our twelve-year-old son Todd, a ten-year-old daughter Stephanie and Sprinter, our large, lovable Golden Retriever who was always on top of the kids and who made a beeline for the entry whenever the doorbell rang.

It was evening and darkness had settled in for the night. Outside a slow cold rain was falling.

"Wouldn't it be fun to have a fire in the fireplace while we watch the VCR movie?" I hinted. Jeff obliged and scurried around until he found some logs that he placed on the gas grate. Soon, golden flames crackled and flickered behind the glass doors, casting a radiant glow on the raised hearth.

The children were excited and had already slipped into their pajamas and sleeping bags that lie directly in front of and below the friendly hearth. Sprinter had snuggled down between them while Jeff and I stationed ourselves on lawn chairs nearby, our eyes trained on the television screen. The house was already beginning to feel like home—so cozy, comfortable and relaxed.

But a short time later we were caught off guard by the sound of someone knocking on the front door. While Jeff and I glanced at each other, Sprinter jumped to his feet, all excited and with his tail wagging.

Since no one in Glen Ellyn knew us, we wondered who could possibly be out in such inclement weather. "I'll get it," I said as I got up.

Jeff hurried to the VCR to stop the movie while the children hung onto their very-hyper puppy who wanted to greet our waiting visitor. There was a lot of movement behind me as everyone moved away from the hearth.

Suddenly, a loud explosion rocked the area around the fireplace. Whirling around, we witnessed the destruction of the safety-glass doors, as they splattered red-hot particles of glass, wood and ash all over the very spot in front of the hearth on which our precious children and pet had been lying only moments earlier.

"Oh, my!" one of us muttered as we all stood there dumb-founded and shocked by what we had just seen happen. The knock sounded again.

While Todd and Stephanie struggled with Sprinter to put him outside, Jeff picked hot debris off the carpet and I went to the front door. Two men were standing outside, their coats wet with raindrops. Softly they asked for a specific address, but being new to Glen Ellyn, I had to excuse myself from being of any assistance. The men smiled, thanked me and calmly retraced their steps back down our long winding sidewalk to the street, a path unlikely that strangers would choose since all of our neighbors homes were better lit, closer to the street and much more accessible for such information.

"Those were angels from God," I exclaimed, convinced by every instinct inside me that we had just experienced a spiritual intervention. Afterwards, when Jeff and I reflected on what had happened, the precise timing of the knock in relation to the explosion, we agreed that God and His angels had truly intervened to save our children and pet from serious bodily harm.

Whether the strangers were Todd and Stephanie's guardian angels in assumed bodies, or merely two human beings that the Lord used as His instruments (the address sought by the men was not even near our house), we are convinced this incident was not a coincidence—unless it was a Blessed Coincidence: the mini-miracle God performs behind our backs to shield us, support us and simply surround us with His love.

Praise Him!

MY ANGEL UNAWARE*

by
Sharon Kay

One cold winter's evening in 1995 as I was driving home from work, headed east on one-way Vermont Street, I stopped for the red signal light at Twelfth. I was waiting in the right-hand lane when a large truck with its blinkers on for a left turn pulled even with me at the light. The vehicle totally blocked my view of Twelfth Street traffic, so when the light finally turned green, I was ready to proceed.

But for some reason, I noticed a young man who had, apparently, been standing on the sidewalk on the far corner to my left. At that exact moment, he decided to cross Vermont Street against the light.

Normally, I would have advanced my car to the center of the intersection and waited for the pedestrian to cross in front of me. But that night, for some unknown reason, I remained in place, wondering first of all, why someone would deliberately cross the street against the light, and secondly, why the truck to my left wasn't turning.

Then, all at once, it became clear! A speeding car coming from the north, and seen by the truck driver, ran the stoplight and passed directly in front of me, over the exact spot into which I would have pulled had it not been for the unexpected appearance of the youth who crossed against the light.

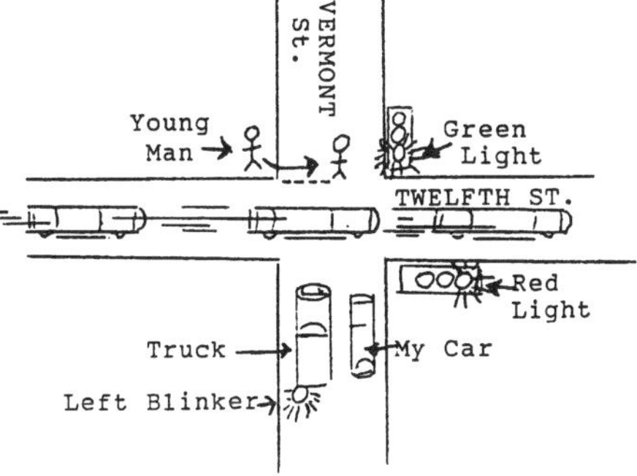

There's no doubt in my mind that I would have been hit broadside and, probably, killed had I not hesitated upon seeing my Angel Unaware, this young man who literally "walked into my life" that night—and saved it.

I instantly thanked the angels outloud for their wonderful and caring attendance.

---

*Angel Unaware: Either a pure angel appearing on earth in an assumed body to complete a mission, or a human being God uses as His instrument to help or save another person.

THREE FOR THE PRICE OF ONE

by
Don Schulte

"Are they not all ministering spirits, sent to serve those who are to inherit salvation?" Heb. 1:14

One day in 1985 when I was employed by the Illinois Veterans Home, I experienced what was thought to be a heart attack. Instead, the doctors discovered that a ruptured colon was sending poison into my bloodstream. Emergency surgery left me with a temporary colostomy.

Afterwards my doctor quipped, "I've buried men with your condition. Lucky for you, that extra pound of fat in that one area prevented gangrene from setting in."

Not long after that, our son Dean was married. My wife Rita and I were proud parents of the groom at the ceremony, but at the reception, I noticed that something was wrong. Not wishing to spoil the affair, I remained silent.

But the following day at our family's reunion, I told Rita about my problem. Of course, she insisted that I tell our daughter who's a registered nurse.

"You should be at the hospital right now, Dad," she advised me. But, once again, I didn't want to interfere with the joy of the reunion. "I'll go in tomorrow," I promised her.

The next day, a Monday, Rita drove me to what was then, St. Mary's Hospital. When we arrived, that's when everything broke loose.

For a week I was a patient in I.C.U. Several times I thought about asking for the Last Rites of the Church, but I kept procrastinating until seven days later when the doctor actually told Rita that she could take me home.

I was relieved to hear the doctor say, "Don's fine now."

But before I could even be discharged and within the hour, I noticed more blood. I told the nurse immediately and she set the wheels in motion for additional surgery.

Rita wasn't on the premises yet, so they prepared me and took me into the operating room before she arrived at the hospital.

When she did walk in and was told of the situation, Rita became upset and pleaded with the personnel, "I haven't had a chance to pray with my husband yet!"

Making an exception for my wife, they allowed her to come into the O.R. in order to pray with me.

"Please, find me a priest," I asked Rita, obviously concerned by the most recent turn of events.

"I'll try, Don," she replied, and once outside the heavy doors, Rita told me she headed for the telephone.

Later, when I finally regained consciousness in the I.C.U. recovery room, I could hear all the usual background noises: voices, footsteps, metal clanking and fans running. It wasn't what I heard that caught my attention as much as what I saw.

From my position, flat on my back, I stared up and into the welcome sight of a priest's face. Then, I noticed another one was there and yet, another clergyman was toward the other side. Not just one—but, there were three priests hovering above me, all looking down. I felt the comfort of a hand resting on my shoulder, and the mere touch of the priest's hand filled me with a feeling of total peace.

For a period of five to ten minutes, the three men of God stood over me, as if protecting me. They did not speak, and I felt no need for words either. Yet, this trio of average-looking clergymen stood there, waiting patiently, as if it were their mission to be there.

I finally decided to rest my eyes. A few moments later when I reopened them, the priests were all gone.

Later, when Rita was allowed to see me, she was about to speak when I felt the need to say, "Honey, I only asked for one priest. I didn't think you were going to get me three." The reaction on Rita's face was one of surprise. "Don, I couldn't even get one," she said quietly, explaining that her parish priests were unavailable, and that the hospital's chaplain could not be located.

Ah, yes! Those wonderful ministering spirits. What do you think?

SAN ANTONIO PICKUP

by
Mary Talken

After Larry's silver-plated frame turned golden in December (See "Anna's Frame"-Chapter 3), I decided that when my youngest daughter Suzy and I went to San Antonio in February, I would stop to pray at the Oblate Fathers' Lourdes Grotto of the Southwest (an exact replica of the

Grotto in Lourdes, France) where masses were being said for our unborn grandchild.

When February 9, 1996 finally arrived, Suzy drove us to the popular Texas town for our mother/daughter weekend. After enjoying the charm of the Riverwalk and reliving the history of the Alamo, we stopped for lunch at a quaint German Pub. When sore feet sent us limping back to our Bed and Breakfast, I called for directions to the Grotto. The brochure I had received from the Oblates showed a picture of the shrine, but gave no address. The woman's instructions were so complicated that I only remembered where to get off the interstate. After that, we would ask directions.

The next day after shopping at the Farmers Market and finishing off a roll of film at the Zoo, we headed north on I-281 and exited on Jones/Maltsberger. Then, we turned left, and pulled into a motel.

The desk clerk directed us back into the same traffic pattern, and after two additional turns, I noticed a familiar name on a sign, Oblate Drive. On the north side of the road was a large brick building, The Oblate School Of Theology.

"But I don't see the grassy hillside described in the pamphlet," I said. "Hey, look! Across the street there's a sign that says, Grotto. Let's try it."

After my daughter maneuvered her car around, we drove south on Grotto Street. But there was no grotto, only houses and more houses, until we reached a T-intersection.

"Pull into that convenience store on the corner," I suggested. While Suzy waited in the Honda, I hurried into the building, the small brochure pressed securely against the palm of my left hand. Several people stood in line, waiting for their turn at the checkout counter.

"Can you tell me how to find this Grotto?" I asked each one as I showed them the picture.

One by one, they shook their head sideways; until, finally, a young man at the end of the line pointed behind himself and said, "The Grotto? It is three blocks that way!"

I thanked him and raced back to where Suzy sat waiting in the car. Praise you, Lord! I thought.

Soon we were cruising down Jackson-Keller. One block, two blocks—no grotto in sight! Three blocks, four blocks, only a school and many houses, and straight ahead, we could see another busy street. Disappointment was testing my faith.

But at the intersection of Blanco and Jackson-Keller, I saw another Fast Stop on the corner. "Let's try one more time," I said, confident that someone here would help us.

Once again, while my daughter waited patiently outside, I repeated my ask-and-point-to-the-picture routine. But this time there would be no help, no young man at the end of the line, and the employee behind the counter was too busy to be interrupted. Oh, Jesus, I thought as I walked back to the car. Please, please help me!

As I sat down, I felt truly heartsick and my spirit fell, along with several tears.

"I know we're really close, Suzy, but I can't seem to find the grotto. We may as well head back to Austin," I sighed. When the car was almost to the curbing, my daughter applied the brakes and suggested that I call the lady who had given us directions a day earlier.

"It's worth a try," I agreed. Suzy turned the Honda back toward the service area and headed for the south end of the same Fast Stop. Two pay phones were mounted on the wall.

With the brochure still clutched in one hand and coins in the other, I started to walk toward the phones. There was no one near me at the time, but suddenly, out of the corner of my right eye, I noticed that someone was coming toward me.

When the stranger, probably in his late twenties or early thirties, was within touching distance, he stopped. He was dressed in the work clothes of someone who did physical labor, and he was holding a set of keys with both of his hands, in front of him and at waist height.

From that moment on, nothing that happened seemed normal or as it should have been, based on my normal life experiences.

"Are you lost?" he asked in the softest, gentlest voice I had ever heard. I sensed immediately that something special was happening.

"Yes, I think I am," I replied, and held the brochure up so the young stranger could see the picture, stepping closer to him in the process. "I'm trying to find the Grotto of . . . "

The man interrupted.

"I'll take you. Come, follow me!" he said, the tone of his voice subdued and almost distorted, his demeanor—so calm and caring, that I wasn't the least bit uncomfortable, even when my Good Samaritan's head seemed extremely close to mine. It was then that I realized that I was in the presence of an angel. His only concern seemed to be taking me to the Grotto of Our Lady. I was overcome with tingles of emotion.

I remember standing there in silence, oblivious of everything going on around me as the stranger turned and, with his back to me, he walked slowly toward a small truck that was parked along the south end of the building. When he was halfway to his vehicle, he glanced at me over his left shoulder and, without saying a word but with one wide-sweeping gesture of his arm and hand, the young man signalled for me to follow him.

I hurried back to the car where Suzy was waiting. "That man's taking us to the Grotto, honey. Follow his truck," I said, realizing that my youngest hadn't the faintest idea of what was taking place. But I did, and I was a nervous wreck.

By now, the truck was waiting opposite our car, facing the busy street behind us. I was still in shock when my daughter made a U-turn and fell into line behind the other vehicle. Then, both drivers pulled out into the busy traffic on Blanco.

At the same time that my brain tried to assimilate everything it had just seen, sensed and heard, I tried to explain it to Suzy.

"I suppose you're going to tell me that's an angel," she remarked, looking straight ahead.

I felt hurt that my own child would question me. I quipped, "Suzy, I'm not trying to tell you anything!" Snapping at my daughter was the last thing I wanted to do, but I needed someone who could share my joy, this unbelievable joy in knowing that we were tailgating a truck being driven by a messenger of the Lord, and not knowing what to do about it. Totally overwhelmed in the moment, I sat fidgeting. Did I remember to say "Thank you!" I wondered.

At Oblate Drive all traffic stopped for the red signal lights. I had an overpowering urge to get out of the car and run up to the cab of the truck. I should wave at the angel! Smile and say "Thank you!" again, to be sure he knows how much we appreciated his help.

But the lights changed to green, and a few blocks later, the half-ton pickup truck in front of us signalled for a right turn. It was then that I saw the small white sign with red letters on a post: Grotto, and an arrow that pointed in the same direction.

We made the turn onto Mount Sacred Heart Road into what seemed to be a construction area of gravel and cyclone fences. As we cruised past one long stretch of the wire mesh, I spotted the green shaded hillside of the Grotto beyond the clutter in the distance.

"There it is!" I cried, ecstatic that we had reached our destination, thanks to an angel in a truck. As much as I wanted to have Suzy blow the horn—something, anything, I couldn't. She already thought I was wacky.

By now my eyes were fixed on the back window of the truck's cab. I was praying for one last glimpse of the heavenly visitor.

Then, I watched in awe as the driver arched his long arm outward and, by using his right index finger, he pointed toward Our Lady's shrine. His arm never waivered, but remained taut and perfectly centered in the window. At the same time, I saw his profile when he turned to face the same direction, as if there was no need for him to watch where he was driving.

When the fence came to an end, Suzy made a right turn into the dusty parking lot and my view of the truck was cut off. By the time I was able to turn myself around to see where The San Antonio Pickup had gone, it was nowhere in sight.

Since Suzy had not been out of her car during the entire incident, she had not heard the man's voice or words, observed his demeanor, or sensed his angelic presence. Because she was totally unprepared for such an encounter, her inability to grasp the moment and its importance is entirely understandable.

Actually, we were almost at the Grotto when we first passed The Oblate School of Theology, but when we made the wrong choice to go down Grotto Street, I imagine God must have shaken His head and said to an angel, "I almost had them there and, now look! They've gotten themselves lost. You'd better help them!" (Picture of the Shrine on cover)

> "Do not neglect to show hospitality, for by that means some have entertained angels without knowing it."
>
> (Heb. 13:2)

ANGELS RIDE BICYCLES, DON'T THEY?

by

Leanne Schell

Several years ago, after having had one breast lump removed, my doctor confirmed the presence of a second nodule. Because my dear mother had died from breast cancer, I was shaken and emotional.

That night a friend of mine and I were to attend a meeting at the Retreat Center on Quincy University's North campus grounds. It was a beautiful summer evening and subtle breezes stirred the lazy green leaves. We both had arrived early, but after my friend took one look at me, she knew that I was in no condition to face a room full of people.

"Let's take a walk," she suggested. But the more we walked and talked, the more I cried, desperately trying to break free of the anxiety that held me prisoner inside.

We were strolling in the shadows, away from traffic and behind the brick buildings when two young girls, riding on bicycles, came toward us. A safe distance in front, they both stopped and straddled their full-sized vehicles, and planted their feet firmly in the grass.

"Why are you crying?" one of the ten-year-olds asked.

Surprised by the sudden appearance of what seemed to be normal youngsters with brown hair and sweet faces, I didn't quite know what to say. Why should they be so concerned about my feelings? I wondered.

"Oh, I'm just very sad right now," was the only response that came to my mind.

"Is there anything that we can do for you?" the second girl inquired.

For a moment, I hesitated. "You could pray for me!" I heard myself saying, and the idea actually sounded wonderful to my ears.

At the time, I fully expected to see the youngsters take off to do their praying later and somewhere else.

Instead, we watched in awe as the pair steadied their bicycles between and with their legs as best they could. Then, with their bony elbows resting on the handlebars, they closed their eyes, folded their hands, and prayed silently—right there in front of us.

"Thank you! Thank you very much!" I told my little friends. "I think I'll go home now."

Suddenly, I realized that my tears had stopped and that a feeling of peaceful relief was coming over me.

As I began to walk toward our old gold El Camino in the parking lot, the girls rode their bikes beside me. Fully intent on cheering me up, they complimented everything from my blouse and shoes to our not-so-wonderful vehicle. I was tickled by the efforts of these two darling visitors who did everything they could to make me, a stranger, feel better. And they had!

After saying goodbye, I watched them ride off, really sorry to see them go.

The next morning my friend phoned me to discuss the unusual experience with the girls. I hadn't been able to get them out of my mind, and by the time we hung up, we both had decided, "We had witnessed angels at work!"

Later that week, my doctor surprised both himself and me when a mammogram confirmed, contrary to his original diagnosis, that the lump had disappeared.

"Amazing!" was all he could say.

Miraculous! was all my heart could say. I knew I had a lot of help, the prayers of so many wonderful friends that could have triggered the disappearance of the lump, along with the question I still keep asking myself . . .

ANGELS RIDE BICYCLES, DON'T THEY?

Well, don't they?

A NEW HEART FOR DEBBIE

by
Rev. Lee and Lavon Amsler
(As told by Lavon)

My husband Lee and I have some precious memories of God's provisions for our Down's Syndrome daughter, Debbie. During the first year of her life, she endured many infections which caused high fevers and congestion. In order to help her breathe easier, I held her up over my shoulder for many hours while I rocked her.

On one particular day, as I was holding her in my favorite living room rocking chair, at a time when she should have been crying because of discomfort, I noticed that she was looking intently up toward the wall behind me and smiling profusely. Because this continued for sometime, I occasionally turned around to see what or, maybe, who she was looking at. But there was nothing to see.

Then, I realized that, perhaps, it was the Lord Himself or one of His angels who was ministering to my child. Debbie was so calm, so serene.

As our daughter grew up, I remember several other unusual things that happened to help her father and I understand how really special she was to God. How much he must have loved our Debbie by revealing Himself and His love for her in so many ways.

When she was thirteen, the doctors told us that our daughter had a hole in her heart, and that probably she wouldn't live any longer than five to ten years. Debbie knew about her heart problem, but she had so much love and faith in God that she told us, "I'm not afraid to die. I'll be in Heaven with Jesus."

Then, in 1993 Lee and I, along with Debbie and her sister, Donna, felt privileged when we were invited by a Belgian missionary to go on a missions tour in Europe. This included some days of rest and sightseeing in Paris. It had already been an exciting trip for seventeen-year-old Debbie. Through an interpreter, she had shared her testimony in several European churches as she told everyone of her love for Jesus and how He lived in her heart. People everywhere seemed drawn to our daughter.

When we reached Paris, we chose to use the city's underground commuter system to see the sights, never realizing how difficult the stairs would be for Debbie. Her body had already slowed down to the extent that climbing steps or having to walk very far would overtax her heart and cause her to nearly pass out.

As we climbed the long staircases between train stops, Debbie became more and more fatigued. Finally, Lee decided to carry her on his back while, occasionally, carrying one or two travel bags in his hands at the same time. Behind them, Donna and I lifted the wheelchair to the top.

In order to conserve Lee's strength, I suggested to Debbie that she might slowly climb every other stairway on her own.

But when we reached the final long staircase, Debbie let out a sigh, "I can't, Daddy. I can't go any farther!" and she tried not to cry.

She stood there, looking so forlorn and exhausted, realizing full well that her father, too, was reaching the breaking point.

"I don't know what to do, Lavon," Lee exclaimed. But knowing my husband, I'm sure that his prayerful thoughts and those of the girls, were rising to Heaven for some sort of intervention.

What ARE we going to do? I remember wondering as I leaned against the hard wall of the dimly lit tunnel, my head resting on my arm. "Oh, Father, in Jesus' name, what do we do now?" I prayed softly to myself. "We need your help!"

All at once, there was a handsome young French-looking gentleman standing in front of us. He was a little taller than Lee and his hair was darker.

"I will carry her up for you!" the stranger said in English but with a slight French accent. He was so calm, soft-spoken and seemed to be interested in only one thing—helping us!

"But she's heavy," I cautioned our Good Samaritan, knowing that Debbie tipped the scale at 120 pounds.

Holding out his right arm, the man patted the jacket material that covered his bicep with his left hand and told us, "I'm strong!"

Then, without another word or asking us any questions, the kind stranger, with no effort whatsoever, scooped our daughter up into his arms and climbed the long flight of stairs effortlessly. When the three of us reached the top with the wheelchair and bags in tow, we thanked our benefactor with all of our hearts.

The young Frenchman nodded and calmly said, "Goodbye!" I tried to watch where he was going as he walked away but, the minute he turned around the gate, he disappeared from sight, just as suddenly as he had come.

Debbie never forgot this incident. It served as an inspiration for her as she told her friends in Europe and back home about it. Her eyes would sparkle, and she seemed to have a greater zest for living, right up to the time of her homegoing to Heaven, a year and a half later, at the age of eighteen years and eight months.

After Paris, Debbie spoke of someday marrying, having a home and having children. She repeatedly mentioned the name of the young man she would marry—a name we had never heard before in Debbie's circle of acquaintances. Could it have been the name she had given to the young man from Paris?

Lee and I had always prayed that Debbie would not be afraid if God chose to take her home. In answer to our prayers, the Lord gave her a beautiful dream six weeks before He took her into His eternal care. Through this dream, our daughter believed there was going to be A New Heart For Debbie. The one she received would last forever; it was the heart of Jesus in which she now rests.

Of course, we cannot be certain that this was actually one of God's messengers, or if another human being was sent to be near us at "just the right time." But if it was an angel, then one day, when we are finally together with Debbie in Heaven, I believe we will meet him there.

We still find it inspiring and amazing that as soon as we called upon the Lord for help, He provided it.

I am reminded of two verses of Scripture from the New King James Version.

> "Call to Me, and I will answer you, and show you great and mighty things, which you do not know."
>
> (Jeremiah 33:3)

> "Call upon Me in the day of trouble; I will deliver you, and you shall glorify Me."
>
> (Psalm 50:15)

Praise God!

~ Chapter 14 ~

Between God and Me

by

____

(Consider writing your story or blessings first on another sheet of paper and recopying it into this book. God bless you!)

~ Chapter 15 ~

The Man Whose Life Was a Miracle

FATHER AUGUSTINE TOLTON

(America's First Black Priest)
Submitted by: Joe Bonansinga

July 9, 1997 marks the 100th Anniversary of the passing of Father Augustine Tolton, our nation's first black priest. Father Tolton pastored a church in Quincy, Illinois for three years before moving to Chicago. This is a man whose life was a miracle.

Augustine Tolton was born on April 1, 1854 in Ralls County Missouri in the community of Brush Creek to Peter and Martha Tolton. The newborn was regarded as the property of slave owner Steven Elliott. With the outbreak of the Civil War, Augustine's father reportedly fled to join the Union Army, as did many others. Augustine's mother, meanwhile, was left to care for three children. Fearing what might happen if she and her children remained in the slave state of Missouri, Martha escaped from servitude, taking the children by boat across the Mississippi River to Quincy.

The post-Civil War era was a very trying time, especially for the Toltons due to racial prejudice. Still, Augustine showed what kind of man he was by pushing toward his goal despite barriers that blocked his path. He had the Lord beside him all the way.

Shortly after coming to Quincy, Father Tolton attended the all-black Lincoln School, and later he enrolled at Saint Boniface parochial school. But because of prejudice, he was forced out of Saint Boniface after one term. He was then admitted to St. Peter's School, headed by Father Peter McGirr, one of Quincy's first integrationists. Father McGirr saw the potential in young Tolton, who was a good student. He showed an early interest in religious matters, and graduated from St. Peter's with distinction.

A number of Quincy clergymen took young Augustine under their wings and tutored him privately. In return, Tolton worked with several local priests to provide for the spiritual needs of Quincy's black Catholics. His education received a major boost when he was permitted to enter St. Francis College, the forerunner of Quincy University. When Augustine showed promise as a potential candidate for the priesthood, the efforts of local priests to place him in U.S. seminaries proved futile because of his race.

Finally, in March of 1880, these efforts paid off when Augustine Tolton was admitted as a seminarian at the College of Sacred Propaganda in Rome. After six years of intensive study, Augustine Tolton was ordained on April 24, 1886, and the following day, he said Mass for the first time over the tomb of St. Peter in Rome. Almost three months later, Tolton said his first mass in Quincy on July 18, 1886 at Saint Boniface. The following Sunday, July 25th, he was installed as pastor of Quincy's St. Joseph Church and its black congregation.

The young priest became well-known for his excellent sermons that attracted people of both races to his church. But prejudicial sentiments and racial pressures escalated, making Father Tolton's stay in Quincy difficult. Finally, he asked to be removed and was assigned to Chicago where he organized a black parish and called it Saint Monica's.

Augustine Tolton continued his service in the Windy City until, at the age of 43, he was felled by a heat stroke in the hot summer of 1897.

Father Tolton, who grew accustomed to adversity during his short life, made it known that he wanted to be buried in Quincy, despite the difficulties he faced there. He is buried in St. Peter's Cemetery at 3300 Broadway. In addition to his grave, a building is named after him, the same building in which the Adoration Chapel is located.

A plaque has been placed in front of St. Boniface Church to memorialize his accomplishments—his miraculous life.

~ Chapter 16 ~

The Chapter of Perpetual Adoration

The pages of our book are coming to a close, but our song of praise and thanksgiving to the Lord goes on forever. Since God is never so close to us as when He personally intervenes in our lives, even in the smallest ways, our fondest wish is that every man, woman and child in the world come to know that closeness—to experience a miracle. God is working in your life; we hope you will watch for Him! Remember how much He loves you.

We hope, too, that you will make use of the special "Between God And Me" chapter to record your own miraculous stories or to simply record the blessings in your life.

Deep in our hearts, each one of us longs for the heavenly touches and reassurances from our merciful and loving God, his Mother Mary and the angels. Perhaps that is why television series, such as Michael Landon's "Highway To Heaven" and the recent "Touched By An Angel" have been so popular. How comforting it would be to know that celestial beings, like TV-characters Tess and Monica, were there to protect and guide us. Our fear of death and the unknown, plus the realization that we humans may not be in control of our destinies, places yearnings in our hearts for the beautiful life promised us for eternity.

Several references have been made regarding our parish Transfiguration Adoration Chapel, and we wanted you to have more information about it. The Chapel was first opened on October 25, 1987, and since that time, there has been someone praying there every minute of the day and night. It takes one-hundred sixty-eight people or more to fill the 168 hour-long slots each week. Not everyone involved is from our parish, but they all come to worship their Lord, Jesus Christ, cheerfully. Everyone who has a regular hour is grateful for it, for in the cozy chapel-room, one can find peaceful quiet, here where God presides from His Blest Host position in the monstrance on the altar. A stack of petition cards rise before Him while fellow worshippers pray for the many intentions.

Without this band of dedicated Christians, and an even more dedicated core group to serve as the backbone, a Perpetual Adoration Chapel would be impossible. But it's worth the effort—remember, the Sacred Heart of Jesus promised us that He would take our names and write them on His Heart, never to be erased, if we help him with Perpetual Adoration. And what blessing will surely come from such an undertaking!

A Chapel Hour is a time of personal prayer, a time to deepen or initiate friendship with the Lord. People may say the rosary, listen to religious tapes, pray from prayer books, reflect on Scripture or speak to God in their own words. Then they listen for His response as they sit and bask in God's love. (There are over 300 such chapels in the United States)

We pray that this book has been a blessing for you. We hope that you will continue to seek the Lord diligently, pray fervently and watch for miracles, interventions and Blessed Coincidences that are happening around you every day of your life. Then, **"LET HIM WHO WOULD BOAST, BOAST IN THE LORD."**

(1 Cor. 1:31)

Come now! As children of a loving God let us continue . . .

. . . . CLIMBING TO PARADISE
(A Prayer For Strength)

Lord, I've never climbed a mountain
quite so tall as what I see
looming like some awkward giant,
reaching up in front of me.

Troubles always came as foothills,
not too big and not too tall,
short enough for crawling over
is my efforts work at all.

But this time I face a mountain
made of solid granite peaks
causing me to shake and tremble
as my voice does as it speaks.

I'll need special strength to climb it . . .
Dear God, be there at my side.
Hold onto the rope above me
should my foothold ever slide.

Give me spikes of trust and courage
so in Faith I'll scale that wall.
Yet be strong when weak and winded
so there's little chance I'll fall.

Pull me up into your sunshine
to a point where I can see
that the Master of the Mountain
always goes in front of me.

For my Master IS forever,
as I will be when I rise
far above these earthly ranges
on my way to Paradise.

There to join with faithful angels
'round the throne of God to sing
songs of glory, praise, thanksgiving,
to our Master, Lord and King!

BIBLIOGRAPHY AND ADDITIONAL READING

Anderson, Joan Wester. *WHERE ANGELS WALK: True Stories of Heavenly Visitors.* Brooklyn, N.Y.: Barton & Brett, 1992.

Anderson, Joan Wester. *WHERE MIRACLES HAPPEN. True Stories of Heavenly Encounters.* Brooklyn, N.Y.: Brett Books, Inc. 1994.

Anderson, Joan Wester. *AN ANGEL TO WATCH OVER ME: True Stories of Children's Encounters With Angels.* New York, N.Y.: Balltine Books, 1994.

Anderson, Joan Wester. *WHERE WONDERS PREVAIL: True Accounts That Bear Witness to the Existence of Heaven.* New York, N.Y.: Ballatine Books, 1996.

Freeman, Eileen Elias. *Touched By Angels.* New York, U.S.A.: Warner Books, Inc., 1995.

Freze, Michael S.F.O. *Voices, Visions and Apparitions.* Huntington, Indiana, Our Sunday Visitor, 1993.

McLellan, Vern. *Quips, Quotes & Quests.* Eugene, Oregon: Harvest House, 1982.

Talken, Mary. *A Walk Upon The Earth.* 1987 *The Whispering Bluffs* (*A Poetic History of Quincy*). 1988 *Of Clowns And Kings.* 1992 (Available: 4014 Prairie Ridge, Quincy, Il. 62301)

ADDITIONAL INFORMATION IS AVAILABLE ON:

The Divine Mercy Message And Devotion, and Blessed Faustina Kowalska of the Most Blessed Sacrament. Call Marian Helpers, Stockbridge, Ma. 1-800-462-7426.

The Fifteen Prayers (revealed by Our Lord to St. Bridget of Sweden), phone MARY'S CALL at 1-816-388-5308 or write P.O. Box 162, 505 College, Salisbury, Mo. 65281 to request the black booklet, "The 4 Keys To Heaven."